The Hindus of Canada

A Perspective On
Hindu Canadians' Cultural Heritage

Ajit Adhopia

1993

Inderlekh Publications,
Mississauga, Ontario, Canada

The Hindus of Canada:
A perspective on Hindu Canadians' Cultural Heritage

The publisher would welcome any information that will enable it to rectify any references or credit in subsequent editions.

Canadian Cataloguing in Publication Data

Adhopia, Ajit. 1940-
The Hindus of Canada

Includes bibliographical references
ISBN 0-9696772-1-9

1. Hindu - Canada. I. Title

FC106.H5A44 1993 294.5'0971 093-093199-8
F1035.H5A44

Published by:
Inderlekh Publications
2546 Pollard Drive
Mississauga, Ontario
L5C 3H1 Canada

Printed at: Narain Press, Noida, India

Laser Type Setting: Vilax Marketing Pvt. Ltd.,
385 Sector 29, Noida-201303, India.

Cover Design & Illustrations: Niraj Sharma, New Delhi.

CONTENTS

The Author

Ajit Adhopia was born in 1940 in Delhi, India. His father, an ardent social reformer of Delhi, had spearheaded during the early fifties an aggressive campaign against prostitution, black marketing in food, and corruption and bribery in government offices. After graduating from the University of Delhi, Ajit emigrated to Britain in 1960, where he was involved in human rights activities. He migrated to Canada in 1968 and became a Canadian citizen. He has been living in Mississauga (Ontario) since 1972 with his wife and two children. He works for the Paul Revere Life Insurance Company as a Rehabilitation Consultant.

Ajit is well known to new Canadians of South Asian origin for his selfless community work and philanthropic activities. He has been involved with many community organizations; he was a founding director of India Rainbow Community Services of Peel, and Asha Jyoti Community Welfare Society of Canada. He is a freelance writer, and has written guest columns on social and political issues in regional newspapers. His feature article *Prejudice and Pride*, published in 1988 in the premier issue of *Mississauga Magazine* was highly acclaimed. He also authored an information booklet, *India to Canada: A profile of Indo-Canadians,* published by the National Association of Indo-Canadians. He is the founder of the first Canadian Hindu periodical *Hindu Dharma Review.* His no-nonsense, hard-hitting editorials on burning social issues cajoled the conscience of his readers. He has offered free courses to Canadian-born Hindu youths to help them understand and appreciate their cultural heritage. He is often invited by schools, churches and community groups as a guest speaker and cultural interpreter for the Indo-Canadian community. He believes that his work *The Hindus of Canada* will serve as a cultural bridge between the Hindu youths of Canada and their parents' culture as well as Canadian Hindus and mainstream society.

FOREWORD

I am extremely pleased and thankful to the Almighty that the author of this book, Ajit Adhopia, has finally been able to fulfil his long cherished desire to write a book on Hinduism for Canadians. The author had long seen the need of explaining the basic principles of Hinduism and Vedic philosophy to the Canadian Hindus who have for the most part forgotten the science of Hindu religion. This book takes care of that need.

I am particularly impressed with its Canadian context. The descriptions of historical perspective, sociological profile of Hindus in Canada, Hindus scriptures, rituals, symbols, festivals, tenets, Sanskaras, customs, and cultural events are lucid, simple, precise and, of course, without prejudice. Throughout the book, the author has kept in mind the need of the readers for whom this book is intended.

The Canadian Hindus have neither time in their fast life nor the will to study their religion in depth. Furthermore, with the many distractions of material life, they have forgotten their own spiritual identity and glorious heritage. This book endeavors to remind them how scientific and logical Hinduism is. While exploring the Hindu mythology in depth, and referencing it where necessary to establish a link between traditional values and modern thinking, the author has remained brief and to the point. Each section is written in such a way that the reader, regardless of his own faith, should be able to examine it independently, rejecting whatever does not suit his reasoning and accepting only what makes sense to him.

The author effectively treats the misunderstanding prevailing amongst non-Hindus about Hindu deities, symbols and rituals, and illuminating the basic truth. This has made the relatively difficult philosophical wisdom understandable even to the ordinary mind. To strengthen his arguments, he has frequently quoted well known Indian and foreign scholars. This has brought credence to his writings.

I have had the privilege of knowing the author, himself a spiritual aspirant, since I started broadcasting a Hindu religious and philosophical radio program in Toronto (Canada) over ten years ago. I am honoured to be associated with the editing of the first draft of this book. Together we have managed to cut down traditional dogmatism to the minimum in order to re-establish the scientific rationalism without over padding.

I must offer my highest congratulations to the author for his tremendous effort and hard labour in writing this much needed book, and keeping our heritage alive in Canada. I hope and pray that the readers will find time to benefit from this book so that the author's labour will come to fruition.

Gyan Rajhans, M.Sc. (Eng.), P. Eng.
Producer and Broadcaster,
Bhajanawali Radio Program,
Toronto, Canada

PREFACE

Why do Hindus consider cows to be sacred ? Is it true that Hindus pray to monkeys, trees and snakes? How many gods do you have? Why do Hindu women wear a dot on their foreheads? These are some of the questions I have been asked again and again ever since I left India in search of a better life, first in England and then in Canada. I had no answers to these questions, as I had never received any formal education in Hinduism. All I knew was that God was everywhere and no one and nothing was more powerful than Him. In grade five, as a part of our social studies, we also read a booklet containing the life stories of Jesus Christ, Prophet Muhammad, Guru Nanak, Buddha, Krishna and Rama. Every time someone condemned or questioned my religion, I felt angry and frustrated. I often wondered why people in the Western world were so ignorant about my religion.

When my Canadian born children were very young, I started taking them to our local Hindu temple to ensure that they learned about their religion. Since the priest recited the Mantras in Sanskrit, and only spoke in Hindi, they did not understand anything. The images of various deities in the temple confused them. They started asking me questions about my religion- e.g. Why does this god have an elephant's head ? Why does this Goddess look so horrible? Which one of these gods and goddesses is the best? My wife and I could not answer their questions; we looked at each other, dumbfounded and embarrassed. We told them not to ask suchsilly questions, and to be quiet. I felt really ashamed of my inability to explain my religion to my children. This is when my quest for knowledge about my religion started.

My children did not speak my language, Hindi, and could only understand simple conversation. My knowledge of Sanskrit is very rudimentary. Being away from India since 1960 adversely affected my ability to fully comprehend the pure and Sankritized Hindi text of the literature I had obtained on Hinduism. With those handicaps, I decided to acquire the knowledge of Hindu Dharma through the medium of the English language. I read many books written by Western authors, and discovered that most of them perpetuated the popular myths the people in the Western world held about Hinduism. On the other hand, the books written by Hindu scholars assumed that the readers already had some knowledge of Hinduism, and expounded deep philosophies of ancient Hindu sages. My children's questions still remained unanswered. I was in a state of confusion until I startedreading the works of Swami Vivekananda, Swami Chinmayananda and Swami Sivananda. I also studied the work of Pundit Nardev Vedalankar, an eminent Hindu scholar from South Africa. The fog started lifting and things illuminated. I discovered that there was a perfectly logical explanation for every thing we Hindus believe and practise. About three years ago, when I started offering a free introductory course to Hindu youths through various temples, I felt the strong need for a book that would explain their cultural heritage in a simple and logical manner. I have tried to explain Hindu religion and culture the way I understand it, and without favouring any particular denomination. I have also presented in a nutshell, a historical as well as sociological perspective on Hindu Canadians, dealing with the stereotypes and popular myths some mainstream Canadians hold about them.

This work is not a textbook on Hinduism or Hindu Canadians; that is why I have not burdened it with footnotes. It may serve the purpose of a popular reading or a primer for any lay person who wishes to acquire a basic understanding of the culture heritage of Canadian Hindus. This has been a missionary project for me. In the process of researching and writing, I have acquired a sense of security and pride in my religion.

ACKNOWLEDGEMENTS

I would like to acknowledge the kindness and voluntaryassistance I have received from some very special persons incompleting this book.

Pandit Nardev Vedalankar: During my quest for knowledge I studied many publications of Veda Niketan of Durban (S.A.), written by Punditji. I was greatly impressed by his style and knack for explaining complex ideas in a very simple way. I was so deeply influenced by his writings that I could not help borrowing heavily from them. I am indebted to Punditji, and express my gratitude for enlightening me.

Mr. Gyan Rajhans: Mr. Gyan Rajhans (of Bhajanawali Radio Program) has been my guiding light, consultant and a positive critic from the day I started writing this book. He edited the first draft with a great sense of dedication. His constructive criticism and immensely valuable suggestions have enhanced the quality of my writing. Above all, he has been a source of inspiration to me. For his selfless contributions, I must thank and salute Gyanji.

Mrs. Gloria MacDowell: Mrs. MacDowell reviewed the initial draft from a non-Hindu Canadian perspective. She also acted as my volunteer copy editor; her sharp pencil and hawkish eyes have polished my work. Her comments, questions, and suggestions were of great value to me. I express my gratitude to Mrs. Macdowell for her contribution.

Ms. Lucy Zita: The second draft was copy edited by Ms. Zita, an English and Art teacher at the Port Credit Secondary School in Mississauga (Ontario). I wish to thank her for giving the final polished shape to my work.

Mr Harish Ahuja (New Delhi, India): In the process of getting this book printed, Harish worked as a link between the printers in New Delhi and myself. Without his efficient and selfless service, I could not have managed to finish the project during my short stay in India.

Shakun, Vik and Preeti: Evenings and weekends are supposed to be devoted to one's family, but I have been depriving my wife Shakun, son Vik and daughter Preeti of this prime family time since I started writing this book. I greatly appreciate their patience, understanding and encouragement. My special thanks to Vik, himself an honours graduate in Political Science with special emphasis on South Asian Studies, for being my consultant and 'resident' editor.

December 22, 1992

Ajit Adhopia
Mississauga, Ontario
Canada

1.

THE ORIGIN OF HINDUS AND THEIR DHARMA

All ancient religions flourished and died as new religions emerged. Although Hinduism is the first religion of mankind, it outlasted all other ancient religions, and is still thriving. Hinduism is an evolutionary religion. Unlike Christianity and Islam, Hinduism does not owe its origins to one prophet. There is no single agency or personality at the root of Hinduism. It evolved over thousands of years on the basis of divine revelations experienced by a series of sages when they were in intense meditation. The divine knowledge thus received by the sages is contained in the four sacred books called the 'Vedas', the fountain head of all Hindu knowledge.

THE MEANING OF "HINDU" AND "DHARMA"

Most Hindus call their religion Hindu Dharma, but in the western world it is called Hinduism. However, it is interesting to note that the word 'Hindu' is not of Indian origin. This word is not found anywhere in Hindu scriptures. There are many interesting stories and explanations about the origin of the word 'Hindu'. Some modern Hindu scholars believe that it is derived from the Sanskrit word 'Hidi' which means to achieve one's objective, to acquire knowledge, to be progressive and ignore what is obstructive. Therefore, a person who follows the spiritual path in order to acquire perfection through divine knowledge is called a Hindu.

However, the most popular story about the origin of the word 'Hindu' is that it is of Persian origin, and has no religious meaning. It is a distorted version of the word 'Sindhu', the name of a river in the northwestern part of India (now in Pakistan) where the early Hindu civilization developed. The ancient Persians referred to Hindus as "people who live on the other side of Sindhu". The story goes that since the Persians pronounced the letter 'S' as 'H', they called Sindhu as Hindu. Thus, they coined the word Hindu for Indian people of that region, and India was then called Hindustan, the land of Hindus. The Greeks transformed 'Hindu' into 'Indus' which finally became India. Some Hindu scholars reject this theory of the word Sindhu becoming Hindu. They assert that ancient India, being amongst the highly advanced civilizations of the world, would not have been without a name; its people were not primitive aborigines waiting to be discovered, identified and named by some foreign adventurer. In 1912, N.B. Pavgee offered a more logical origin of the word Hindu in his book *Self-Government in India.* He states that a Sanskrit scholar, Swami Mangal Nathji, had found ancient Hindu writings called Birhanaradi Purana, in the village Sham of district Hoshiarpur in Punjab. It contained the verse, "Himalayam Samarabhya yavat bindusarovaram Hindusthanamiti qyatam hi antaraksha-rayogatah." When translated this means, "The country lying between the Himalayas mountain and Bindu Sarovar (Cape Commorin sea) is known as Hindusthan by combining the first letter 'Hi' of Himalayas and the last compound letter 'ndu' of the word Bindu.

The meaning of Dharma

The ancient Hindus called their religion 'Dharma'. In English, the word Dharma is translated as Religion, but in fact the English language has no single word to give the true and complete meaning to Dharma. It comes from the Sanskrit word *Dhr* which literally means *to sustain* or *to hold together,* and has a much more comprehensive meaning: Dharma includes all moral and social obligations, virtues, codes of behavior, right actions, traditions, and beliefs that sustain human life on earth.

Many Hindus also refer to their religion Sanatana Dharma.

In the Sanskrit language, Sanatana means eternal, ever existing or everlasting. The truths it expounds are eternal and everlasting. Since the Vedas are considered the ultimate source of all knowledge, some Hindus prefer to call their religion Vedic Dharma.

THE ANCIENT ANCESTORS OF HINDUS

How old is Hinduism? How did Hindu society evolve over the centuries ? To answer these questions the Indologists have written much literature. This very complex and controversial subject is outside the scope of this book. The chronology of Hinduism and the evolution of Hindu society is extremely difficult to pinpoint. An average Hindu is more concerned with what their Dharma is than how old it is. However, the sources of information about the evolution of Hindu society are the historical accounts pieced together from archaeological findings, inscriptions, the writings of some foreign travelers and the knowledge derived from Vedas and Puranas consisting of traditional stories.

THE INDUS VALLEY CIVILIZATION

The orthodox Hindus claim that Hinduism and their society is ageless or as old as human race. However, most historians start the account of Hindu society from a highly developed ancient civilization discovered by the series of archaeological excavations which started in 1917 and are still continuing. The historians call it the Indus Valley civilization as it arose in the lower Indus River Valley spreading from Sindh (now in Pakistan) to Gujarat, Punjab, Himachal Pradesh, Delhi and Utter Pradesh. The Harappa and Mahenjodaro culture, named after the sites of excavations, started somewhere between 3000-2500 B.C., although the most recent findings seem to push the date to around 6000 B.C.

The exact racial origin of the Indus Valley people is not known, but the facial features of the figurines seem to indicate they were a dark skinned race, probably the ancestors of the present day Dravidians of South India. The spectacular archaeological findings reveal that it was a highly evolved urban society. The people of this wonderful ancient Hindu civilization knew the use of gold, silver, copper, tin, lead and bronze. They had constructed large hill citadels consisting of living palaces, public baths, modern looking lavatories and granaries. The two storied and spacious brick houses in the town lined the well planned streets; the underground sewer system reflects the existence of some sort of efficient municipal government. The food stuff found includes wheat, barley, fruit, meat and fish. They grew cotton, and practised weaving and dyeing activities. They had skilled tradesmen and merchants. Harappan merchants traded with ancient Egypt and other middle east countries.

The Indus Valley Hindus left behind many works of art that included terra-cotta toys, beautiful pottery, and steatite seals with intricately engraved animal and female figures and with a line of pictographic script. The writings deciphered in 1956 would indicate that their language was structurally similar to the present day Dravidian language of South India, but this view is not acceptable to many historians.

The seals and figurines strongly suggest that the people of the Indus Valley civilization had some sort of religious order. The figures of a meditating Yogi, Lord Shiva and Goddess Shakti connect their religion with the modern Hindus. The huge public bath, 40 feet by 23 feet, dug out at the Mahenjodaro site would suggest that they gave high priority to personal hygiene and ritual bathing which is still a part of the Hindu lifestyle.

THE ARYAN INVASION THEORY

How the great Indus Valley civilization disappeared is still a mystery, and a subject of much dispute and debate amongst archaeologists and historians. The western historians have been promoting the theory that the tall and fair skinned Aryans were responsible for ending this civilization. They believe that the Aryans invaded Northwest India repeatedly but they were able to subdue the Harappan people by 1500 B.C. According to their theory, the Aryans belonged to the great Aryan family of seven races- Hindus, Persians, Greeks, Romans, Celts, Teutons, and Slavs- who emigrated from their ancestral home in Central Asia to Europe and India. The Hindu Aryans originally settled in the valley of the Indus, developed a great civilization and spread to the eastern and southern regions of India.

A CHALLENGE TO THE ARYAN INVASION THEORY

Many modern scholars reject the Aryan Invasion theory, and call it a myth manufactured by piecing together some circumstantial evidence. Many Hindu scholars have condemned it vehemently, but it remained unchallenged in the Western world until recently. The Aryan Invasion is indeed a theory but it has been perpetuated in the western history books for so long that it has been accepted as a historical fact. Therefore, it is important that we briefly discuss the new challenge to the traditional theory.

The Aryan Invasion theory was popularized in the mid 19th century by Max Muller, a German philologist and Orientalist who became a Sanskrit scholar and interpreted many Hindu texts. He used this theory in order to explain why many words in European languages and north Indian languages had common roots. It gained more credence after the Indus Valley civilization was discovered, and became a handy tool in explaining why this great civilization disappeared. Until then, the expression Arya or Aryan never had a racial connotation. Hindus had believed that India was always the ancient home of the Aryans and the term 'Arya' or 'Aryan' did not refer to any racial group; it meant 'someone who is noble or civilized'. According to this body of opinion, ancient India was populated by various indigenous racial groups. Although each group had its own set of customs and traditions based on varying geographical, environmental and historical factors, they all had a common religion. The mixture of various races was known as Aryan society with no racial connotation whatsoever.

Most recently, Professor Subhash Kak, Professor N.R.Warhadpande and Dr. S.P. Gupta, Prof. David Frawley and many other scholars have done considerable research to disprove the Aryan Invasion theory. Dr. S.P. Gupta points out that the Indus valley civilization was initially declared non-Aryan and pre-Aryan for three basic reasons: 1. the absence of horses; 2. the absence of iron; and 3. the presence of cities. However, Dr. Gupta argues, further excavations at several important Indus valley settlements have yielded bones of domesticated horses; the fact that the Rig Veda refers to metals, particularly copper, as Ayas does not mean that the Indus Valley culture and Vedic culture were not one and the same. Dr. A.R. Kennedy, an expert on physical anthropology, asserts that the terms Aryan and Dravidian have cultural origins, and anthropology cannot identify any human skull as Aryan or Dravidian.

In his book 'Gods, Sages Kings', Dr. David Frawley of the USA has also resoundingly debunked the Aryan Invasion theory. He concludes that the Aryan people were in fact the creators of the great Indus Valley Civilization. He quotes extensively from Vedic hymns to prove that the Vedic people lived in the Himalayan region and came down to the plains due to heavy floods caused by drastic climatic changes. His research and interpretations of Vedic hymns indicates that the so called Aryan Invasion was in fact a civil war between two groups of Aryans; the people who practised spiritualism through rituals, and the 'fallen' people who had given up such values and practices as they were corrupted by materialism; each side was supported by kings and leaders of different races that lived in India. He also refers to the new findings in the excavation at Dwarka (now in the Gujarat State) indicating that "a large stone port flourished around 1500 B.C. and presents an urban development intermediate between the Indus Valley sites and the time of the Buddha. These sites appear to be definitely Aryan and show the oldest form of Brahmi script, the alphabet of ancient India. These show that Aryans were building great cities, had an alphabet and were engaged in maritime trade at the time they were supposed to be just entering India as primitive nomads."

Again, according to Prof. Warhapande, the so called conflict between dark-skinned people and whites was not a racial war; it was a conjecture or a literal translation of some hymns in Rig Veda. For example, when the Rig Veda said that Lord Indra flayed the 'dark skin' to protect the Aryans, it was a metaphor for forces of darkness, a cosmic term. Like many other cultures, in Hindu culture darkness represents ignorance or wickedness and the white colour is a symbol of purity or righteousness. Even today, we use such expressions as black market, black leg, black day, and black sheep. The supporters of Aryan Invasion also claim that the Aryans later adopted many aspects of the Native culture. This is also an illogical argument. History has shown that the conquering people impose their own culture on the conquered people. The European settlers in North America did not adopt the native culture. They called the natives savages, and the Christian missionaries tried to 'civilize' them by imposing western values and beliefs. The missionaries in India also called Hindus 'pagans' and tried to 'redeem' them. The Muslim invaders did exactly the same thing in India. If Aryans were foreign invaders, why would they embrace the natives' culture and religious practices ?

According to Professor Kak, "The archaeological evidence about the Saraswati river provides a chronological framework. Literary references in the early Vedic literature compel the conclusion that before this river dried up its settlements were of the Vedic people. But the settlements before drying up are those of the Harappans." Both Professor Kak's and Professor Frawley's research conclude that the Saraswati valley area was the main centre of the great Vedic civilization and it pre-dated the Indus valley culture. Since Vedic people were very spiritual, they called themslves Arya (Aryan) which means noble, and does not refer to a racial group.

AN OVERVIEW OF INDIAN HISTORY.

Regardless of the correct meaning of the word Aryan or the true racial identity of the Aryan people, their religious beliefs and practices came to be known as Arya Dharma. The ancient Aryans, established settlements and a rich agricultural economy. They built social, educational and religious institutions many of which have lasted until today. They developed many republics and mighty kingdoms- Magadha, Maurya, Gupta, Chera, Chola and Pandya- the ruins of which still stand today, oozing with the glory of ancient Hindus. The highly prosperous India also attracted many other foreign invaders and settlers who were gradually integrated into the Hindu mosaic. Most notable among them were Greeks, Huns, Shakas and Kushanas. When Alexander, the Macedonian conqueror, invaded India in 327 B.C, it was already a highly advanced society. His invasion opened the door to a Greek influence on Hindus. In turn, through the Greek connection, Hindu thoughts and culture penetrated the West.

The glory of ancient India lasted until 800 A.D. when Hindu society started decaying and mighty empires were fragmented into hundreds of weakened, tiny kingdoms. The period of 800 A.D to 1300 A.D is referred to as the 'dark age' when political disintegration encouraged the powerful invasions by Turks, Arabs, Afghans and Persians. The successive waves of Muslim hordes butchered civilians, destroyed Hindu temples, plundered India and returned home with caravans loaded with wealth and women. Later Muslim invaders stayed, established their rule and built empires in India starting from the last quarter of the 12th century. In 1398, India was invaded by the Mongol bandit-conquerer Timur with his cavalry force of 90,000. Timur's ruthless and ferocious soldiers massacred civilians while he proclaimed himself as king.

Muslim rulers, with some notable exceptions, called the Hindus 'infidels' and oppressed them with their harsh treatment and contemptuous behavior. A special tax, called Jaziyah, was imposed on the Hindu population. Hindus' holy books were burned. The famous library full of ancient Hindu scriptures and precious manuscripts of literature, located in the holy city of Banares, was reduced to ashes. Hindu idols were trashed, temples were demolished and mosques were erected on their sites. Many Muslim rulers engaged in forced conversion of Hindus to the Islamic faith. It is this pattern of behavior which is largely responsible for creating the animosity that many Hindus harbor towards Muslims even to this day. Under the rule of the famous Moghul emperor Akbar, Hindus enjoyed some relief from oppression. The Islamic rule in India made a profound impact on every aspect of Hindu culture. Many Moslem practices and traditions were adopted by Hindus. Islamic art, literature and architecture heavily influenced India over a period of 500 years.

The British replaced the Moghul empire in India. During the British rule in India that lasted for more than 150 years, Christianity also made a strong imprint on Hindu culture. The British rule ended in 1947 when India was partitioned. A separate Muslim country called Pakistan was formed.

Despite the heavy onslaught of foreign influences, the core of Hindu beliefs and thoughts was kept intact by a succession of saints, sages and socio-religious reformers. It is believed that the wondrous Hindu stamina for interegration and absorption is also responsible for the survival of Hinduism.

"Grassroot Democracy"-A Village Council Scene *[ref .pg 10]*

2.

THE SEEDS OF DEMOCRACY IN HINDU SOCIETY

Western history books and encyclopedias tell us that the concept of democracy was born in ancient Greece where City-States were first established around 700-600 B.C. However, this claim may seem shaky to those who have researched and studied the Hindu polity and discovered the first seed of democracy in the soil of ancient India. According to A.L. Basham, "In any case modern India may take legitimate pride in the fact that, though they may not have democracies in the modern sense, government by discussion was by no means unknown in her ancient civilization." Many examples of ordinary citizens electing an individual to govern their country is found in the first Hindu Scripture Rig Veda, and other ancient literature.

"The people have chosen the ruler"

Rig Veda, 10-124-8

"The wise men have selected a king"

Atharva Veda, 10-3-5

"that king follows the wishes of the people, and governs according to the dictates of the people"

Atharva Veda, 15-9-1

"He who has the peoples' approval becomes king; he who does not have the approval cannot be king"

Satpatha Brahmana, 9-3-2-5

ANCIENT DEMOCRATIC INSTITUTIONS

THE ELECTED KING

During the early Vedic period, each tribal settlement was governed by a chief who was called Raja. The Raja was elected primarily as a military leader. His function was to protect the kingdom from foreign invasions and to establish internal law and order; in return, the citizens gave him certain privileges and a fixed portion of their harvest; he was also allowed to retain a portion of the war booty. A contract existed between the Raja and his electors; his role was to please the people who elected him, and as a head of the government, he was a social servant.

SABHA AND SAMITI: THE ASSEMBLIES

Originally, the Raja was not an absolute monarch, as the affairs of the kingdom were governed by two assemblies, Samiti and Sabha. Samiti means "meeting together"; Sabha means a body of men "shining together". The relationship between these two constitutional bodies is not very clear. Some scholars claim that the two names were inter-changeable and were used to describe the popular assemblies that developed side by side in different parts of ancient India. The Atharva Veda describes them as the two daughters of the Prajapati (Creator). However, many indologists believe that the Samiti was a popular assembly of ordinary citizens that elected the Raja, and renewed his term, while the Sabha was an exclusive council or advisory body of elder statesmen. This two-tier ancient democratic institution of the Hindus can be considered the fore-runner of the modern Canadian Parliament and the Senate.

The Raja was required to attend the sessions of both Samiti and Sabha. Apart from electing the king and dealing with the political issues, Sabha was also an assembly of people that discussed the matters related to the distribution of wealth, both for religious, war and secular purposes.

GANAS: THE HINDU REPUBLICS

The term Gana means "an assembly of co-habitants" or "rule by many" Some historians believe that Hindu republics existed before the elected monarchial system of government while others speculate that the republics were set up in the North-East hilly region by the Aryan migrants of Punjab who rebelled against the Vedic orthodoxy. Regardless of the controversy about its origin, it is generally accepted that the republican system of government, mostly in the North-East regions, co-existed with the monarchial system. The epic of Mahabharata (Santi-Parva Ch. 107) also acknowledges some republican chiefs' participation in the great war. The Jain and Buddhist literature amply attest to the existence of republics. Buddha himself was the son of the chief of a republic. The account of the famous foreign traveler Meghasthenes also makes clear references to this democratic tradition.

The main feature of the republican system was its corporate character. The political process involved the meeting of the heads of households in a public assembly hall. The assembly was presided over by an elected chief whose title was not hereditary. Public issues were debated and voted upon if no clear consensus emerged. The republican chief also acted as the principal executive officer and ran the administration of the republic with the help of his cabinet of assistants who were also elected by the assembly. The Eastern republics espoused Buddhism and accepted the foreign invaders- Greeks, Shakas, Kushanas and Huns- into their fold.

As the elected monarchy became hereditary and was accorded divinity by the Brahmin orthodoxy, the ambitious kings started attacking the republics to expand their kingdoms. These republics gradually disappeared after 100 B.C. but some inscriptions and coins confirm the survival of some until 500 A.D.

PANCHAYAT: THE VILLAGE COUNCIL

As the tribal settlements evolved into villages and the

boundaries of kingdoms expanded, the structure of the popular assembly also changed. Since it was no longer practical for the entire population of the kingdom (Rashtrya) to meet, the principle of representation came into being. The village became a political unit, and the village head, Gramini, represented his people in the Sabha. The Atharva Veda makes references to the Gramini attending the coronation ceremony. When the institutions of Sabha, Samiti and republics disappeared, the village council (Panchayata) became a democratic institution by itself. In most kingdoms of ancient India, the village council was not recognized as a part of the formal government structure. There is no indication that the rights and power of the village council were derived from a royal charter; the village council always functioned independently of any influence from the rulers.

In some parts of India, the village council, traditionally consisting of five venerated elders that included their head (Sarpanch or Mukhia), was elected by the village folks. In the South, the composition varied according to the local customs; in some regions, the entire adult village population attended the meetings of the village council but the executive powers were delegated to an inner cabinet; in other regions, the village was governed by a number of committees elected by the adult population. It must be emphasized that the village council was a community agency and its members did not receive any remunerations, and could be impeached for biases or misconduct. Regardless of its composition, the village council managed the social affairs and civic amenities although in some parts, it also became a revenue assessment and collection agency for the king, an arbitration board for civil disputes, and a people's court for social crimes. The council's decisions on disputes were only morally binding, but were generally honoured. Any ordinary citizen could request the council head to call a meeting to deal with any matter of concern, either personal or common.

Grass root democracy in the form of a village council has survived up to the modern age, regardless of the political turmoil and chaos that has taken plaee in India over the centuries. Since independence, the structure, responsibilities and the authority of the Panchayat system have been enhanced.

FREEDOM OF EXPRESSION

The freedom to express one's thoughts and propagate them, a key ingredient of democracy, was enshrined in the Vedas long before the concept of freedom of expression became a cliche in Western society. Logical scrutiny, discussion and investigation of its beliefs is not only permitted in Hinduism but encouraged and welcomed. Every Hindu has the right to question and criticize his religious beliefs without the fear of any reprisal or being accused of committing a blasphemy; no one has ever been burned alive on a stake, ex-communicated or declared as a non-believer for contradicting the beliefs of his religion.

In this context, it is interesting to note that Galileo, the famous 17th century Italian mathematician and astronomer, was forced to repent by the Roman Catholic Church, and remained under house arrest for eight years for saying that earth revolved around the sun; this scientific truth was contrary to what the scriptures had stated. It took a Vatican commission 13 years of deliberations before Galileo was found "not guilty" by Pope John Paul II in November, 1992. In contrast, consider the case of a Hindu atheist scholar, Charvaka, whose violation was lot more serious than Galileo's 'crime'. Charvaka founded a nihilistic school of thought in ancient India. He vehemently denied the existence of God, the authority of Hindu scriptures, and repudiated all doctrines. His followers, called Nastikas, asserted that there was no life after death, no world beyond this world, religious ideas were delusions, and moral values were mere convention. They preached avoidance of pain, pursuit of pleasure, and freely promoted the *eat, drink and be merry* approach to life. Some Hindus wonder whether the current generation in North America is following the way of life prescribed by Charvaka's followers. Neither Charvaka nor the Nastikas were persecuted nor suffered any dire consequences at the hands of Hindu orthodoxy. In fact, much of Charvaka's literature is still available to inquisitive Hindus. Had Galileo been a Hindu in ancient India, he would not have been treated so harshly.

The following verses in Atharva Veda serve as warning to the ruler who violates his people's right to speak freely:

" O King! the speech made by the learned ones was not to be suppressed. O powerful king! do not desire to suppress the speech of the learned ones as it cannot be silenced."

Atharva: 5-18-1

" The speech of the learned ones is banned. It wishes to express itself but it has been stifled. Such a suppressed voice becomes more dangerous and militant. "

Atharva: 5-18-3

"The king suppresses the voice of the learned one. He drives out the spirit of militancy and force from him. The king then wishes to destroy the learned one. He imprisons him. But in reality by doing so the king is digging his grave."

Atharva: 5-18-4-44

In modern India, the largest democracy in the world, the right of freedom of expression, enjoyed by people of all religions, is enshrined in the constitution. India has a very lively and free press. Hindus are very proud of this democratic tradition and zealously guard it. In 1976, when the Prime Minister of India, the late Mrs. Indira Gandhi, suspended all human rights and imposed a harsh emergency rule, she suffered a humiliating defeat in the following general election.

EQUALITY

It is a myth that the concept of equality was invented in Europe or North America. The following verses from Hindu scripture will shatter this much publicized myth:

" No one is superior or inferior. All are brothers. All should strive for the interest of all and should progress collectively."

Rig Veda

"All have equal rights in articles of food and water. The yoke of chariot of life is placed equally on the shoulders of all."
Atharva Veda

" This our motherland gives equal shelter to people speaking different languages and following different faiths."

The inequality inherent in the caste system is not condoned by the Vedas. In fact, the caste system itself is an aberration of the Varna system which treated the people of all occupations equally. Many Hindu reformers, including Mahatma Gandhi, have strived over centuries to eradicate the evils of this distortion of the Hindu ideal of equality. The caste system is dealt with elsewhere in this book.

On the political level, the concept of equality remained the prisoner of foreign rule, including the British, for centuries until it was reintroduced in independent India. The Indian constitution gives equal rights to all citizens of India, regardless of sex, caste, colour, creed or religion.

TOLERANCE

Democracy cannot survive without practising tolerance towards people with opposing viewpoints. Traditionally, tolerance has been a hallmark of Hindu society. According to Hinduism, all paths lead to the same destination, and all faiths and religions are these paths. This belief has made Hindus tolerant and respectful towards other religions.

Like Canada, India has been a safe haven for people who came to its doors to escape persecution in their own countries. Other faiths and religions of non-Indian origins have grown and flourished in India. The Jews have been living peacefully in India for 2000 years. When they first came to India to escape persecution in the land of their origin, not only were they received with open arms by ancient Hindus, they were allowed to practice their faith. The Hindu rulers of Kerala gave them land and money to build their synagogues. The magnificent synagogue of Cochin, built in 1568, is a testimony to Hindu tolerance.

In the early 8th century, when the people of Zoroastrian faith (known as Parsees) in Iran were persecuted by Muslim crusaders, they took shelter in India. The first group of Parsee refugees settled in Delhi and then in Gujarat and Maharashtra. Today, the Parsees are one of the best educated, most prosperous and highly respected community in India.

Christianity arrived in Hindu India before it took roots in Europe. Soon after Christ was crucified, one of his twelve disciples, St. Thomas, came to South India to preach the Gospel. Now, the population of Indian Christians of all denominations exceeds the entire population of Canada. The landscape of India is dotted with elegant ancient churches. Christmas is still a public holiday in India.

The peaceful Islamic preachers had won converts in India and established some Muslim settlements along the West Coast before the Muslim hoards from Arabia invaded to loot and plunder India. Today, after Indonesia, India has the second largest Muslim population in the world. In 1947, Pakistan was carved out of India to create a separate country for Muslims, but the number of Muslims who voluntarily chose to remain in India exceeds the entire population of Pakistan.

In recent years, unscrupulous political leaders have started using religion as a tool to gain power and their militant activities have triggered much violence. In the Canadian media, such violent incidents have been focused on heavily and over-played while the above stated testimonies about the tolerant attitudes of Hindus remain unpublicized. The fact that the vast majority of Hindus live in peace and harmony with their non-Hindu neighbors also fails to make headlines in Canadian media. Had the Hindus been an intolerant and violent people, minority religions would not have survived and flourished in India. Had the Hindus been militant, after independence, they would have made India a Hindu State instead of a secular democratic republic.

Freedom of expression, tolerance, non-violence and the synthesizing of conflicting viewpoints are still the main pillars of Hinduism- without them Hinduism itself would not have survived the onslaught of so many aggressive and powerful alien forces.

3.

THE CLASSIFICATION OF HINDU SOCIETY

THE FOUR VARNAS, CLASSES

Man is a social being with the natural desire to belong to a group. After satisfying the basic needs- food, shelter, clothing and physical safety- the desire to seek social affiliation becomes stronger. Since people differ in nature, they tend to associate with a social group of like minded people. It is evident even today when people join formal or informal occupational groups, social or recreational clubs, professional associations and trade unions. Within the same religion, people also belong to different denominations and attend different churches or temples. This basic nature of human beings gave birth to the Varna system in ancient Hindu society. The Varna system catered to all three human needs- social, occupational and religious. It is believed that the caste system evolved as an aberration of the Varna system. There are various theories about the origins of the Varna system.

THE TRADITIONAL THEORY

Being mindful of man's social needs, the ancient Hindus classified society into four major groups which came to be known as the four Varna: *Brahmins* (priests and intellectuals), *Kshatriyas* (rulers and warriors), *Vaishyas* (merchants and traders) and *Shudras* (artisans and manual workers). The Sanskrit word Varna has its root in the word *Vriyn* which means *to choose*. In this way, each member of the society is free to choose a livelihood and occupation according to his aptitude and attributes. The Varna system had absolutely nothing to do with one's birth, race, colour or creed. Historians believe that it was designed to deal with the chaos that was created when ancient India was in the process of being transformed from a tribal society to a developed and settled civilization. According to some historians, the Varna system was only a theoretical framework to establish a social order by division of labour, and create a proper balance in socio-economic activities which was later sanctified by the Vedas.

THE THREE GUNAS THEORY

According to Hindu philosophy, the universe has been created by three *Gunas* (attributes): *Satoguna* (balance and equilibrium), *Rajoguna* (action or motion) and *Tamoguna* (inertia). People also possess these three qualities in varying degrees which are reflected in their characters and instinctive preferences for certain activities. In the beginning, the satoguna dominated human character and activities. As the human race evolved, individual preferences for activities changed and economic realities also compelled this change. Consequently, vocational activities became diversified; people chose different occupations based on their attributes and inherent tendencies. People with similar preferences emerged as distinct social groups. This was an inevitable process in the socio-cultural evolution of the human race.

Hindus believe that this natural phenomenon, known by different names, is to be found in every society of the world. Any society can be divided into four broad categories:

1. Intellectually inclined people e.g. teachers, priests, writers, lawyers, social reformers, and thinkers etc. Hindus called them Brahmins.

2. People who govern, legislate, protect the society and maintain the law and order, e.g. politicians, administrators, judges, police officers and soldiers etc. Hindus called them Kshatriyas.

3. People who produce material wealth, e.g. shopkeepers, businessmen, merchants, traders, bankers, investors

industrialists and salesmen. Hindus called them Vaishyas.

4. People who provide manual labour and skills to the society, e.g. carpenters, blacksmiths, plumbers, factory workers, weavers, potters and other artisans or craftsmen. Hindus called them Shudras.

Equality in the Varna system: The Vedas compared society with the body of a person. Yajur Veda (31.9) poses some questions about this person, the society: " What is the face of this person, what are his arms, what are his stomach and thighs and what are his feet? " These questions are answered in the following verse (31.10): " Brahmins are the face of this person, the arms are Kshatriyas, the stomach and thighs are Vaishyas and the feet are Shudras."

The concept of equality of the four classes, the organs of the society, is inherent in this analogy. All organs are equally important for the proper functioning of the body. Similarly, all four Varna, classes, have equal status, none is superior or inferior. Each organ of our body is meant for specific functions which cannot be performed by the others.

Mobility in Varna system: Mobility from one class to another was the main feature of the Varna system as ancient Hindus were not Varna conscious until the much maligned caste system emerged later on. The evidence of mobility is quite clear in Smriti literature. Even the sage Manu who is often accused of transforming the Varna system into a hierarchy, approved of mobility. According to the Manu Smriti (10.65), "the son of a Shudra may attain the rank of a Brahmin if he were to possess his qualifications, character and accomplishments, and as the son of a Brahmin may become a Shudra who sinks to his level in his character, inclinations and manners; even so must it be with him who springs from a Kshatriya; even so with him who is born of a Vaishya." The other Smriti literature also allowed the change of Varna due to other reasons under the section *Apad-Dharma* (duty when in distress); when a person cannot follow the occupation of his Varna due to a legitimate reason, he is allowed to earn his livelihood by pursuing other trades or professions. Indian history cites many famous Brahmin and

Shudra as rulers and warriors (Kshatriya).

THE RACIAL THEORY

A common stereotyped Western view on the social division of the ancient Hindu society is based on a racial theory. Many Western historians tell us that the people of white race, called Aryans (or Arya) from Central Asia invaded India and conquered the dark skinned natives, mostly Dravidians. Since the Aryans considered the dark skinned natives an inferior race, the former devised the Varna system of four classes, in order to maintain their racial purity. They substantiate this theory by pointing out that the Sanskrit word Varna means colour. They claim that the early Aryans were divided into three classes: warriors or aristocrats, priest and common people- and created the fourth servitude class of Shudras for conquered Dravidians who were relegated to doing menial tasks and serving the three superior Aryan Varnas. This Western concoction, also accepted by some English educated Indians, created social disharmony and political unrest as the light skinned Hindus of North India started considering themselves superior to the dark skinned Dravidians of the South. After India became independent, some misguided politicians of the South used this social alienation caused by Northern Chauvinism to justify their demand for a separate country for Dravidians. Abroad, many politically motivated racist organizations, including Klu Klux Klan in the USA and the Western Guard in Canada, have exploited this erroneous theory. They claim that the white Aryan conquerors lost their glory, and became impoverished because they did not retain their racial purity. The progressive modern scholars vehemently condemn the racial connotation of the Varna system. According to S.V. Ketkar:

"For centuries, till the arrival of European scholars on Indian soil, the people of India never meant by the word 'Arya' that race of invaders who reduced the natives of the soil to servitude. The word indeed probably had such a meaning, but only for a short period antedating the concrete beginnings of civilization in India. Before the close of the period of the composition of Rig Veda, the descendants of the invading tribes had forgotten where they came from, and thought themselves to be autochthonous (original inhabitants) and men of noble qualities and culture. The word 'Arya' had received some sanctity, and had become rather a title to be applied to properly qualified people, than a word expressive of the recently-born conception of race."

In his work *The Wonder that India Was*, Basham describes the assimilation of Aryans and aboriginal people in the very early stage of the development of Hindu society:

"For all the rigidity of the class system the Brahmins soon lost their racial purity, and it has been suggested that, as Aryan culture expanded, the schools of aboriginal sorcerers and medicine men managed to obtain a footing in the Brahmanic order, just as aboriginal chiefs were certainly assimilated to the warrior class. This may well be, (since) the proto-Hinduism of the Harappa culture was ultimately assimilated to the Aryan faith."

In modern India, one can easily prove the absurdity of grouping Hindus by race or skin colour, by merely looking at the numerous racial, physical features and skin colours people have in every caste and region. It is not uncommon to find dark skinned people among the so called upper castes and the people with fair skin among Shudras. One cannot identify a Hindu's caste by his physical features or the colour of his skin.

THE CASTE SYSTEM

The caste system in Hindu society has both intrigued and repulsed people in the Western world. This social institution has received so much bad press in North America that giving it a fair hearing or presenting both sides of the coin becomes a very difficult task. This is what we are attempting in this section.

Every Hindu belongs to a *Jati* which means caste. Today, Hindu society is divided into over three thousand castes . Some Hindu scholars believe that the caste system has nothing to do with the non-hereditary four Varna. Others claim that numerous social groups pre-existed the Varna system which was simply an effort to group them under the four broad categories. For example, Bhattacharyya points out, "Where numerous races meet and mingle, it is possible to synthesize them in a greater society by placing them in four basic castes."

According to a third school of thoughts, over the centuries, the Varna system became rigid, hierarchical and hereditary, and the caste system is the product of mixed marriages between the people belonging to the four Varna. When the offsprings of the mixed marriages of four Varna lost their social status on both sides, they formed a separate caste outside the pale of the Varna system. When some members of this newly formed caste married the members of another caste or Varna, say Vaishya or Kshatriya, their offsprings emerged as a separate caste when they were disowned by both sides of the family. In this manner, the original four Varna kept on multiplying through inter-marriages.

Pandit Nardev Vedalankar, a Hindu scholar of South Africa, offers four major factors that led to the transformation of the Varna classification into the castes system as we know it now:

1. "**Profession and occupations-** People of different occupations formed different associations each of which had members who shared a common interest just as we have the trade unions these days. Each group kept its trade within the family. Since then caste came to be based along family lines."

2. "**Difference in Place-** People of one occupation lived together in one settlement as one caste. When some of them moved out and settled in another town or district they identified themselves as sub-caste, e.g. Brahmins who settled in Kanoj called themselves Kanojia Brahmins."

3. "**Lineage and Family-** People of a family or household began to be proud of their descent particularly when

they were endowed with advantages by birth. They considered themselves to be superior to others. Gradually, the emphasis of a person's worth shifted from occupation to birth."

4. "**Foreign Association-** Over thousands of years many tribes came into India. They all settled in the country and accepted the Hindu faith but there were differences in their customs and traditions. This led to the formation of numerous castes based on birth. They too had pride in their race and this again gave rise to high and low caste.

The historians find it impossible to trace the point at which the caste system started emerging from the Varna system. However, it must be emphasized that the Varna system is validated by the Vedas whereas the casteism is considered a distortion of the former, and not sanctified by the Vedas. The caste system has been an evolutionary social institution; new castes emerged and many old ones disappeared due to socio-economical and political changes. Each caste that followed a specific trade or occupation developed its own customs, rituals, codes of social and moral behavior and rules governing their economic activities. Each caste was a self-sufficient unit and met all the needs of its members-social, cultural, economic and political. The people belonging to the same caste but living in different regions held regular conferences to discuss common issues and amend their rules in a democratic manner. It sounds like a great cooperative idea to organize a society, but the principles on which the caste system worked transformed the Hindu society into more than three thousand social islands with no bridges to connect them.

THE CASTE BARRIERS AND DISCRIMINATION

Practically, the caste system operated on three basic rules; 1. one must marry within one's own caste; 2. one must not share food with a person of another caste, especially with a person of a lower caste; 3. one must live by the trade or profession of one's own caste. Over the centuries, the caste system became extremely rigid and discriminatory. The caste consciousness and hierarchy generated a sense of superiority and inferiority which weakened the main pillars of Hinduism- equality, freedom and tolerance- and ruined the Hindu society. The Brahmin lawmakers, supported by the Kshatriya rulers, developed very harsh laws that discriminated against the women and the people of lower castes, particularly Shudras. The punishment for the same crime was harsher for the people of lower castes. Inter-caste marriages became a taboo. A person was judged by the characteristics of his caste, often pre-conceived, and not by his personal qualities. A casteless person had no identity or status. The caste system became so rigid that it was impossible for an individual to improve his status outside his caste unless his entire caste was upgraded by the Brahmin orthodoxy. Although economic conditions forced the acceptance of occupational mobility, the caste structure still remained intact. People who left the occupation of their caste were still considered members of the same caste. For example, if a Shudra became a teacher, he could not be upgraded to a Brahmin; he would still be considered a low caste Shudra and followed the social norms of his own caste. In most societies, the upper class people with power and wealth have oppressed and mistreated the people at the lower rung of the economic ladder. This is what also happened in the Hindu society.

THE WORST VICTIMS, UNTOUCHABLES

The Hindus who fell outside the pale of the four Varna system were called *Achhoot* or *untouchables* on account of the lowly tasks they performed, e.g. latrine cleaners, street sweepers, cobblers, scavenger and tanners, etc. These people had absolutely no rights or status in society. They were subjected to the most humiliating and inhumane treatment by the three upper castes, particularly by the Brahmins. Shudras were treated even worse than the African slaves in America. They were considered impure and any physical contact with them was considered polluting. A Brahmin would take a bath if he accidently touched an Achhoot. They were required to live outside the village. They had a very wretched existence and lived at the mercy of the members of the upper castes. Economically, they suffered the worst type of exploitation; in return for their services they only received discarded clothes and stale food. When physically abused, they would not dare complain to the law enforcing authority due to fear of reprisal or lack of action; as such agencies were run by people from upper castes. They were told that their status was the result of their bad Karmas in their previous lives. They could only improve their next birth by working hard and living a pious life.

Although the caste system cannot be justified on the basis of the norms and standards of the 20th century, considering its antiquity, it was not a very strange system as it evolved during the time when other societies in the world (including Europe) were too primitive to even think of establishing any type of social order. Most societies in the world practised social segregation in one form or the other until recently. The English class system worked, more or less, along the same lines. In seventeenth century Sweden, any person marrying outside his class was severely punished. In Germany, if a member of the noble class married a woman of a lower birth, civil law deprived her and her children from inheriting his property. We all know about what Hitler and his concept of the superior race did to Jews. The legal segregation of Afro-Americans of the USA until very recently, the apartheid system of South Africa and the exclusion of the Canadian Native people from mainstream society are other examples of a class system which was no different than the Hindu caste system. Even the communist system in the former Soviet Union failed to create a classless society. Therefore, the caste system is not an historical anomaly.

POSITIVE CONTRIBUTIONS OF CASTE SYSTEM

In retrospect, despite the injustices, human suffering and the damage caused to Hindu society, the caste system did make positive contributions to the evolution of Indian civilization. It served as a vehicle for transforming India from a tribal society to an established civilization at a much earlier age than any other society in the world. It removed the social and economic chaos caused by the transition. The caste system, a better substitute for a tribal grouping, created a social and economic security system. Every member was assigned a place and a role to play in the society. It provided cultural freedom and economic security. A caste was like a trade union or a guild. By following his ancestral occupation, every person received free training in the family trade and was guaranteed a livelihood.

The shield of the caste system protected the society from the social upheavals caused by constant political turmoils. The foreign invading tribes and new immigrants were easily assimilated into Indian society as each new group was assigned a Varna which later became a caste or a sub-caste. For example, the Hun invaders settled in Northern India, mostly in Punjab, and became a caste in the Kshatriya Varna. This is how the Late S. Radhakrishnan, ex-President of India and a renowned philosopher, summarized the contribution of the caste system to the development of Indian society:

"Caste was the answer of Hinduism to the forces pressing on from outside. It was the instrument by which Hinduism civilized the different tribes it took in. Any group of people appearing exclusive in any sense is a caste. Whenever a group represents a type, a caste arises. If a heresy is born in the bosom of the mother faith and if it spreads and produces a new type, a new caste arises. The Hindu society has differentiated as many types as can be reasonably differentiated, and is prepared to accept new ones as they arise. It stands for the ordered complexity, the harmonized multiplicity, the many in one which is the clue to the structure of the universe."

Throughout the centuries, many Hindu saints, sages and social reformers condemned the caste system as an un-Hindu institution because it contradicted the Hindu ideals of freedom, equality and tolerance that are enshrined in the Vedas. Indian history is full of movements that tried to free the Hindu masses from the shackles of the caste system. Buddhism's efforts to eradicate casteism ended when it became a minority religion. Sikhism condemned casteism, and tried to promote a casteless society but had a limited success; its adherents still practise a modified version of the hierarchical Hindu caste system. Sikhs are divided into four major castes- Khatri, Jat, Ram-Garhiya and Majahabi. They rarely inter-marry, and each groups sets up its own separate temple. Many Hindus, particularly of low caste status, embraced Islam and Christianity in an effort to escape the oppressive and discriminatory caste system of Hindu society. But they too carried the baggage of their caste loyalty and pride into the new religions. For example, the Muslims whose ancestors were Hindu Rajputs still take great pride in their Rajput heritage.

CASTE SYSTEM IN MODERN INDIA

Caste consciousness and loyalty became so deeply ingrained in the Indian psyche that it could not be erased by any political system although most educated Indians paid lip service to the evils of the caste system. Even the British made no attempts to eradicate its abuses and inequalities. In fact, they used the caste rivalries to their political advantage. The British Indian army had formed regiments along religious and caste lines. They played one religion against the other, and one caste against the other using the principle of divide and conquer.

In Independent India, the solution to the caste problem was found in educating the masses and economic progress. With the spread of education and economic gains resulting from rapid industrialization, the tight grip of casteism has loosened over the educated urban population: the inhumane practice of caste pollution and impurity to which the low caste people were subjected has more or less disappeared; in choosing a career, caste is not a relevant factor at all; inter-caste marriages are not uncommon, and carry no social stigma; people of all castes socially interact freely. However, the progress in the villages has been very sluggish due to a low level of education.

CORRECTING THE HISTORICAL INJUSTICES

Independent India, being a secular country, did not abolish the caste system. However, the negative aspects of casteism were totally incompatible with the basic principles of modern democracy and Indian constitution. Under the Indian Charter of Rights, it is illegal to discriminate on the basis of gender, caste, creed, race, religion and place of origin. They also realized that outlawing the discrimination alone would not improve the socio-economic status of low caste Shudras and untouchables. Since independence, a large number of social welfare programs and economic initiatives have been introduced for their benefit. For example, 22.5 % of all jobs in the federal government are reserved for untouchables and the people of aboriginal tribes, now classified as Scheduled castes, scheduled tribes. The same quota applies to admissions to all government funded universities where they receive free education. In parliamentary elections, a certain number of constituencies are reserved for candidates from the aforementioned two categories. Recently, efforts were being made to increase this percentage to 50%, and include in the quota system the people of some more historically disadvantaged lower castes, called Backward Classes.

In this manner, correcting the historical injustices and exploitation inflicted upon the weakest section of Indian society has been a national priority for every successive government in India. In modern India, the low caste Hindus and former untouchables have become organized and assertive. They wield enormous political clout, and every political party tries to woo them for votes. As a result, they have produced lawyers, doctors, elected politicians, cabinet ministers, engineers, judges, ambassadors, professors and successful businessmen. Prior to independence, such professions were held exclusively by the people of the three upper castes. For example, the current Vice President of India, a highly educated and exceptionally qualified person, belongs to an Untouchable family. In contrast, one wonders how long it would take to have a black or Native Indian Prime Minister in Canada. In less than 50 years of independence, the most disadvantaged people of Indian society have made more progress than the native people of Canada have in 200 years. Perhaps, Canada can learn some lessons from India in this respect. Will any government in Canada have the political will and boldness to introduce such legally enforceable policies and programs to improve the status of native people, women and visible minorities as has been done in India ?

4.

HINDUS' CONTRIBUTIONS TO SCIENCE

Like most people in the West, Canadians know very little about the marvellous achievements of the ancient Hindus and their contributions to world civilization. The average Canadian seems to think that the entire world was primitive until Greek and Roman civilizations emerged. In recent years, some interest has developed in the cultures of ancient Egyptians and Chinese, but the marvels of ancient India are still waiting to be introduced to Canadians. This chapter is a humble effort in that direction.

TESTIMONIES TO HINDUS' ACHIEVEMENTS

The Hindus of ancient India, then known as Bharat or Aryavarta, developed a highly prosperous and advanced culture long before the birth of Greek and Roman civilizations. Not only did they evolve great philosophies, they excelled in every aspect of human endeavor: international trade, public administration, poetry, literature, visual arts, medicine, grammar, mathematics, astronomy and aeronautics. Many Western scholars who explored the ancient Hindu culture found a treasure of knowledge that surpassed all other civilizations of the world. Outlined below are the observations of some of these Western scholars.

"A system which is in some respect almost identical with that thought out by Spinoza and the profoundest thinkers of modern Europe. Indeed, if you will pardon the anachronism, the Hindus were Spinozas more than two thousand years before the existence of Spinoza, and Darwinians many centuries before Darwin, and Evolutionists many centuries before the doctrines of evolution had been accepted by the Huxleys of our time, and before any word like Evolution existed in nay language of the world."

Monier Williams

"The resemblance between Hindu and Greek philosophy is too close to be incidental. The Hindus being far more advanced, must have been the teachers and the Greeks the disciples."

B.Count

"In the philosophical monuments of India, we discover so many truths and truths so profound, making a contrast with the meanness of the results at which the European genius has sometimes stopped, that we are constrained to bend the knees before that of the East and to see in this cradle of the human race the native land of the highest philosophy."

Victor Cousin

"We British people are not cleverer than the Hindu: our minds are not richer or larger than his; we cannot astonish him, as we astonish the barbarian, by putting before him the ideals that he never dreamt of. He can match from his poetry our sublimest thoughts; even our science perhaps has few conceptions that are altogether novel to him."

Professor Seeley

"If there is any place on the face of this earth where all the dreams of living man have found a home from the very earliest days, when man began the dream of existence, it is India."

Rolland M. Romain

"The influence of that civilization worked out thousands of years ago in India, is round and about us, every day of our lives. It pervades every corner of the civilized world. Go to America, you will find there as in Europe the influence of that civilization , which came originally from the banks of Ganges."

M. Delbos

"It was India's mighty religion that formed her claim to greatness amongst the world's people. Rome has passed and left her ruins; Greece has passed and left her literature; India older than Greece and Rome- India that was old before Egypt was born- India that was ancient before Chaldea was dreamt of- India that went back thousands of centuries before Persia had come to the front- India was still a living nation, when the nations of the past were dead, and their dust had vanished from the surface of the Globe."

Annie Besant

HINDUISM AND SCIENCE

Hinduism contains more than just metaphysics, mythological stories, rituals and a series of commandments to regulate human behavior; it is a complete system to sustain human life on this earth. Hindu sages and scholars of ancient India were obsessed with the quest for knowledge, both spiritual and non-spiritual. They observed every phenomenon around them and investigated it objectively to discover the truth behind it. This unquenchable thirst to discover the truth resulted in many discoveries related to theology, social science, political science and physical sciences which are found in their holy scripture called the Vedas which literally means Knowledge. No human or divine knowledge is outside the scope of Vedas. Ancient Hindus found no conflict between science and religion; such a conflict is purely a recent phenomenon. According to the Hindu viewpoint, religion and science complement each other. This attitude led them to many scientific discoveries to which modern man should be indebted. The Spanish Muslim author and teacher of science, Said al-Andalusi (born 1029 A.D.), acknowledges in his work "The Book of the Categories of Nations", the contributions to science of all known nations of the world. This is how he views India and its people:

"The first nation to have cultivated science is India. This is a powerful nation having a large population and a rich kingdom. India is known for the wisdom of its people."

"They are people of sublime pensiveness, universal apologias and useful and rare inventions."

MEDICINE

Although the Western world recognizes Hippocrates (460-370 B.C.) as the father of the modern medical science, the evidence of the first medical knowledge is found in Hindu texts, Atharva Veda and Kausika Sutra of 1000 B.C. Hindu physicians of the 6th century B.C. had already developed a highly remarkable system of medicine and surgery; they described ligaments, sutures, lymphatics, nerve plexus, fascia, adipose and vascular tissues, mucous and synovial membranes and many other muscles. In 500 B.C. the Hindu surgeon Susruta was the first one to do skin grafting; he had grafted on a torn ear a portion of skin taken from another part of the body. The works of Susruta and Charaka on medicine are well known to Hindus. Ayurveda, the ancient Hindu medical system, still flourishing in India, has recently been introduced in Canada and the USA. Many Western scholars have acknowledged the ancient Hindus' contributions to medical science.

"Ancient Hindus attained as thorough a proficiency in medicine and surgery as any people whose acquisitions are recorded"

Prof. Wilson
(Wilson's Works, Vol III, p. 269)

"Indian medicine dealt with the whole area of the science. It described the structure of the body, its organs, ligaments, muscles, vessels and tissues. The Meteria Medica of the Hindus embraces a vast collection of drugs belonging to the mineral, vegetable and animal kingdoms, many of which have now been adopted by European physicians........ The surgery of the ancient Indian Physician was bold and skilful. They conducted amputations arresting the bleeding by pressure, a cup shaped bandage, and boiling oil "

"The Hindu medicine is an independent development. Arab

medicine was founded on the translations from the Sanskrit treatises made by command of Khalif of Baghdad (950-960 A.D.). And European medicine down to the 17th century based upon the Arabic, and the name the Indian physician, Charaka, repeatedly occurs in Latin translations of Avicenna(Abu Sina), Rhazes (Abu Rasi) and Serapion (Abu Sirabi)."

Dr. Sir William Hunter

The earliest hospital opened in Europe was in the 10th century but Hindus were the first to establish hospitals for the general public. A detailed account is recorded by Fa-Hsien, the Buddhist Chinese traveller who toured India during the years from 405 to 411, and visited a public hospital in the eastern city of Patliputra (modern Patna).

CHEMISTRY AND METALLURGY

The earliest composition of Vedas indicates that Hindus were using metals including copper, zinc, lead, tin , ore, and gold during the Vedic age. The Atharva Veda and Yajur Veda make references to smelting technology.

According to the history of chemistry in Europe, Paracelsus (1493-1541 A.D) was the first one to introduce the chemical knowledge to medical science when he used mercury for internal administration. The history of Hindu chemistry is much more ancient. In his work History of Hindu Chemistry Vol.1 , Elphinstone states:

"Their chemical skill is a fact more striking and more unexpected..........We have indeed reason to suspect that Paracelsus got his ideas from the East.......The Hindus are entitled to claim originality in respect of the internal administration of metals generally, seeing that the Charaka and the Susruta, not to speak of the later Tantras, are eloquent over their virtues."

The use of vaccination, first introduced to Europe in the 18th century, is found in the writings of Dhanvantri, the ancient Hindu physician. Dhanvantri described how animal vaccination can be secured by transmission of the small pox virus through the cow.

ASTRONOMY

Ancient Hindus had developed the knowledge of astronomy long before the birth of Galileo. Western scientists who have studied the works of the ancient astronomers of India, have acknowledged that the Greeks and Arabs were the disciples of Hindu astronomers. According to Weber, astronomy was practised by Hindus as early as 2780 B.C but Davis believes that the first Hindu astronomer, Prasara, lived around 1391 B.C. Other famous Hindu astronomers were Aryabhatt, Varahmihira and Bhaskaracharya. The following excerpts from the works of various Western scholars clearly indicate that Hindus were the world pioneers in astronomy.

"During the eighth and ninth centuries the Arabs were, in astronomy, the disciples of Hindus, from whom they borrowed the lunar mansions in their new order, and whose Siddhants, they frequently worked up and translated in parts."

" In some points the Brahmins made advances beyond Greek astronomy. Their fame spread throughout the west, and found entrance into the Chronicon Paschale (started about 300 A.D. and revised under Heraclius 610-641 A.D.) "

Sir W. Hunter

"It is highly probable that the knowledge of the twelve signs of the Zodiac was derived from India"

Dr. Robertson

" (Aryabhatta first introduced) Diurnal revolution of the earth on its axis, and to have known the true theory of the solstitial and equinoctial points."

Chamber's Encyclopaedia

"The science of astronomy at present (19th century) exhibits many proofs of accurate observations and deduction, highly credible to the science of the Hindu astronomers. The division of the ecliptic into lunar mansions, the solar zodiac, the mean motion of the planets, the procession of the equinox, the earth's self support in space, the diurnal revolution of the earth on the axis, the revolution of the moon on her axis, her distance from the earth, the dimensions of the orbit of the planets and the calculations of eclipses are parts which could not have been found amongst an unenlightened people."

Prof. Wilson

ARITHMETIC

Hindus always had great fascination for arithmetic. Modern day science is indebted to ancient Hindus who invented the concept of zero and the decimal system. Without the concept of zero which is the basis of the Binary system, computer science could not have taken birth. Modern numerals which are used throughout the world are the product of Hindu genius and were passed on to the Europeans through their Arabian contacts. In the Arabic language a digit is called Hindsa which means *from India.* The Arab historian, Hasan Al-Masudi, confirms the Hindu origin of modern numerals:

"A congress of (Hindu) sages at the command of the creator Brahma invented the nine figures, and also their astronomy and other science."

Many western scholars and historians of mathematics (like Prof. G.P. Halstead, Prof. Ginsburg, Prof. De Morgan, Prof. Hutton, to name a few) acknowledge the above Hindu contributions to the world.

"The Hindu notion was carried to Arabia about 770 A.D. by a Hindu scholar named Kanka who was invited from Ujjain to the famous court of Baghdad by the Abbasid Khalif Al-Mansur. Kanka taught Hindu astronomy and mathematics to the Arabian scholars; and with his help they translated into Arabic the Brahmasphuta Siddhanta of Brahma Gupta. The recent discovery of Hindu numerals was well-known and much appreciated in Syria about the middle of the 7th century A.D."

Prof. Ginsburg

"During the eighth and ninth centuries A.D., the Indians became the teachers in arithmetic and algebra to the Arabs, and through them, to the nations of the West. Thus, though we call the latter science by an Arabic name; it is a gift we owe to India."

Schlegel

"To them (Hindus) we owe the invention of the numerical symbols on the decimal scale. The Indian figures 1 to 9 being abbreviated forms of initial letters of the numerals themselves, and the zero, or 0, representing the first letter of the Sanskrit for empty (sunya). The Arabs borrowed them from the Hindus and transmitted them to Europe."

Sir W.W. Hunter
Imperial Gazetteer, P.219 "India"

ALGEBRA

The inquisitive and analytical minds of ancient Hindus developed algebra concepts which are in use even today. This is how Colebrooke summarizes their prowess in this field:

" They (Hindus) understand well the arithmetic of surd root; they were aware of the infinite quotient resulting from the division of infinite quantities by cipher; they knew the general resolution of equation of the second degree and had touched upon those of higher denomination, resolving them in the simplest cases, and in those in which the solution happens to be practicable by the method which serves for quadratics; they had attained a general solution of indeterminate problems of the first degree; they had arrived at a method for deriving a multitude of answers to problems of the second degree from a single answer found tentatively.

"Many other western authorities also accept the originality and superiority of the Hindus' knowledge in algebra:

"Equally decided is the evidence that this excellence in algebraic analysis was attained in India independent of foreign aid."

Manning

"To the Hindus is due the invention of algebra and geometry and their application to astronomy."

Prof. Monier Williams

"There is no question of the superiority of the Hindus over their rivals in the perfection to which they brought the science. Not only is Aryabhata superior to Diaphantus but he and his successors pressed hard on the discoveries of the algebraists who lived almost in our own time."

Elphinstone

"The astronomical, Truti to time measures about the thirty-four thousandth part of a second. This is of special value in determining the exact character of Bhaskaracharya's claim to be regarded as a precursor of Newton in the discovery of the principle of the differential calculus, as well as its application to astronomical problems and computations. This claim is indeed far stronger than Archimedes's to the conception of a rudimentary process of integration."

Dr. Ray

GEOMETRY

Hindus cultivated and excelled in the knowledge of geometry long before the Arabs and Greeks. For example, the concept called Surya Siddhanta consists of a rational system of trigonometry, totally different from what was first known to Greeks and Arabs. This system is based on a geometrical theorem which was not known to the European geometricians until two centuries ago. It employed the sines of arcs, unknown to the Greeks who used the chords of double arcs. Many people in the West believed that sines were invented by Arabs, but the Edinburgh Encyclopaedia states that it is possible that they learned this improvement in trigonometry from Hindus.

According to Dr. Thibaut, the geometrical theorem of the

47th proposition, Book I, which is traditionally attributed to Phythagoras, was solved by Hindus two centuries earlier.

The following excerpts from Elphinstone's History of India attests to the ancient Hindus' mastery over the geometrical skills that were later discovered by Europeans.

"Their geometrical skill is shown among other forms by their demonstrations of various properties of triangles, especially one which expresses the area in the terms of the three sides and was unknown in Europe till published by Clauvius, and by their knowledge of the proportions of the radius to the circumference of a circle, which they express in a mode peculiar to themselves, by applying one measure and one unit to the radius and circumference. This proportion, which is confirmed by the most approved labours of Europeans, was not known out of India until modern times."

AERONAUTICS

One would be astounded to learn that ancient Hindus had highly advanced knowledge of aeronautics. The most ancient Hindu scriptures, Vedas, make clear references to air travel. Other literature- Ramayana, Mahabharata- also give glowing description of a flying vehicle called Vimana. Such references cannot be dismissed as science fiction or poetical fantasies. Sage Bhardwaja, probably the first solar scientist, outlines in great details the technology to build both military and commercial aeroplanes in his works Yantra Sarvasva and Brhad Vimana Sastra. These vehicles were driven by solar energy and their speed ranged from 1000 miles an hour to 20,000 miles an hour. The technology to utilize solar energy is described in his outstanding scientific work Amsubodhini Sastra, which gives an exhaustive analysis of the properties of Solar Rays.

Sage Bhardwaja's books on pure science and aircraft technology have been known to the Indian scientific community for more than three decades. Scientists of the Indian Institute of Technology at Bombay have been conducting experiments to check the validity of Bhardwaja's scientific knowledge and achievements in the field of solar energy and aeronautics. In their first experiment, they studied a component of an instrument, Chumbakmani. On the basis of the formula described in Brhad Vimana Sastra, they were able to produce a shining black substance which has been known as soft ferrite and semi-conductor material. In another experiment, they reproduced a solution called Pargrandhikadrava by Bhardwaja. This solution is sensitive to light and changes colour when exposed to solar radiation. The materials produced in the two experiments are components of an instrument (described as Guhabarbhadarsa Yantra) of an aircraft. Further evaluations of Bhardwaja's work are still in progress at the Indian Institute of Technology.

Hindu Canadians are very proud of their legacy of outstanding scientific achievements by their forefathers. The achievements of Hindu scientists working in Canada and the USA are proving that their thirst for knowledge is as intense as that of sage Bhardwaja.

5.

HINDUS ABROAD

Hinduism did not remain confined to the boundaries of India; in ancient times, it spread to distant lands. Before the birth of Christianity and Islam, Hinduism was practised by the people of Burma, Malasia, Indonesia, Thailand, Cambodia, Laos, and Vietnam. For about a thousand years, 700 B.C. to 300 A.D., Hinduism held sway in these countries. Although most of these people now follow other religions, their names, villages, customs, arts, drama and festivals bear the strong imprints of Hindu culture. Even today, the stories of *Ramayana* and *Mahabharata* are part of their culture.

Over the last two centuries, Hindus also migrated to Mauritius, Fiji, Suriname, Guyana, Trinidad, Burma, Sri Lanka, Uganda, Kenya and more recently to Canada, USA and Britain. It is estimated that there are about 816 million Hindus scattered around the globe; Hindus live under almost every flag. It is also estimated that by the year 2001, the population of Hindus in the world will represent one-sixth of the entire human population on earth. For inquisitive readers, a complete list of countries with Hindu population is provided in an appendix at the end of this book.

HINDUS IN ANCIENT AMERICAS

The Canadian and American children learn at school that America was discovered by Christopher Columbus in 1492. The people of Iceland claim that Leif Eriksson, the Viking explorer of Norway, landed on Canadian soil in 1000 A.D. The Irish people say that this credit should go to an Irish monk, St. Brenden, who first landed on American shores around 500

A.D. There are a number of scholars in the world who have produced some very convincing evidence that the Hindu Aryans from India, along with Chinese and Central Asians, colonized the Americas during the pre-historic times. Many historians have found traces of the ancient Hindu culture clearly visible even today in the customs and traditions of indigenous people of the Americas; the Incas of Peru, Chibchas of Columbia, Mayas of Central America and Aztecs of Mexico. The similarities between Hindu culture and the culture of native Indians of South and Central America are too awesome to be considered coincidental or mythological. Although a detailed analysis of the vast body of literature available on this subject may be outside the limited scope of this booklet, we will briefly talk about the thoughts and conclusions of some scholars.

Dr. I. M.. Muthanna of British Columbia says in his work *The people of India in North America,* "There are numerous instances on record concerning the political and religious leaders of India of the hoary past, having had gone to Europe, America and other countries on political and religious missions. Rishi Vyasa with Sukhdev, probably, 5000 years back, went to America and lived there for some time."

The famous French Indologist, Mon. Delbos who did comparative studies of various ancient cultures, also reached the same conclusion:

"We thus find, the Hindu civilization over-ran the entire universe and that its landmarks are still to be seen all over the globe."

The records of ancient India indicate that the Hindus had good knowledge of world geography and also possessed the technical know-how to travel to distant lands on political, religious and trade missions. In his work *The Primitive Traditional History*, Hewitt writes, "Hindu merchants brought to Mexico the 18-month year of the Hindu *Pandavas.*" According to Hindu scholars, South America is called the *Patal Loka* in ancient Hindu literature, and Argentina was named after *Arjuna*, the famous hero of the great *Mahabharata* war, who conquered that region and married princess *Alupi*, the daughter of the defeated ruler.

In May 1988, the UNI published an article in which the author claimed that the Hindus of Indus Valley and Vedic civilizations had close links with the Mayan people of Mexico. This report described in detail the amazing similarities between the two ancient cultures. According to the Hindu historical texts in *Puranas,* the *Pandavas* rulers had invited the Mayan architects to participate in the construction of their royal court at *indraprastha* (modern Delhi).

A tablet discovered during the excavations of the ancient mounds in 1841 in Cincinnati, Ohio, gives a reliable clue to link the religion and culture of the ancient Americans with the Hindu civilization of India. According to Alex Del Mar, the statues found in those mounds were of Krishna or Buddha, and were probably made by a Hindu artist of ancient America. The natives of South and Central America believe in the Hindu concepts of Mother Earth, transmigration of soul and incarnation of God. Chaman Lal, a Hindu scholar, observes that the American Indians worship Hindu deities *Ganesha*, *Surya* and *Indra,* follow the system of priesthood, casteism, marriage, cremation, *sacred thread* ceremony and other rituals of Hindus. In his book *Hindu America*, he quotes the Mexican scholar Sqeir:

> "The Buddhist temples of South India and of the islands of the Indian archipelago, as described to us by the learned members of the Asiatic society, and numerous writers on the religion and antiquities of the Hindus, correspond with great exactness with those of Central America."

The founders of the Inca dynasty of Peru claimed to be of Ayar Brahmin of India. In his work *Les Races Aryan de Pary*, the Spanish scholar states, " Every page of Peruvian poetry bears the imprint of the *Ramayana* and the *Mahabharata.*" The Peruvian state language, *Quenchua*, has Tamil and Sanskrit phonetics and semantics. Lopez has compiled a collection of one thousand such words. The Hindu musical instruments have been preserved by the Peruvian national museum in Lima. A pillar found in Ecuador bears an inscription which has been identified as a variant of *Brahmi*, a script of ancient Hindus. The Curator of the National Museum of Mexico, Professor Raman Mena, asserts: "The (Mayan) human types are like those of India. The irreproachable techniques of their reliefs, the sumptuous head-dress and ostentatious buildings on high, the system of construction, all speak of India and the Orient."

If we accept the theses of the scholars who make the cultural and linguistic connection between the ancient India and the natives of the Americas, the next logical question involves how the Hindus reached here. Many eminent historians and geologists claim that the Bering Strait did not exist in the ancient times and Alaska was never glaciated. As a result, there was a free movement of people from Asia to Americas. The two great migrations to America took place in 9800 B.C. and 2300 B.C. According to Dr. Muthanna, "Those American Indians of the earlier times were originally the Asians and they entered the continent through Alaska and then settled along the coasts of British Columbia, Oregon, California and Central America." The excavations in the Fraser Canyon indicate that the British Columbia interior was populated around 7000 B.C. as this region had become free from ice by 7500 B.C. The Hindus must have been among those early Asian immigrants as many modern indologists believe that the Mount Kailash in Tibet was the original home of Aryans.

However, some modern indologists claim that the ancient Hindus came to Americas by sea. These interpreters of ancient Hindus scriptures produce the evidence that the Aryans of ancient India were maritimers, and not nomadic people as portrayed by most earlier western scholars. The most prominent among such modern scholars is David Frawley of New Mexico who has done very impressive research into the geography of the Vedic times. Frawley claims that Vedas are a product of a maritime culture as the theme of ships, ocean and the long journeys across the seas permeate the Vedas, the most ancient scriptures of mankind. The Vedic seers urged their people to go abroad by sea and air in order to propagate their philosophy and culture. This is evident from this verse in Yajur Veda:

"Oh men, those who are fit to do administrative work righteously go to the seas in the large fast going steamers, and to the high heavens in steamships or air ships built scientifically. Let mankind of the different countries of the world acquire knowledge from learned men born in this country, India."

The concept of ancient Hindus being adventurous maritimers is also reinforced by Pomponious, a Roman Chronicler of Julius Caesar's time. He wrote about the accounts of Mettulus Celer who was a pro-consul in Gaul around 62 B.C. Celer reported that he was offered several Indians as a present from the King of Suevans. Upon inquiring about the origins of these Indians, he was told that they belonged to the Indian seas, having been carried by high winds across intervening seas. Dr. Muthanna states, "The route to America that was used by Hindus seem generally to have taken place through the sea route from the east coast of India or from Sri Lanka. They set out along the Bay of Bengal to Java, Borneo and Bali and thence to America after stopping at those numerous islands of the Pacific. They seemed to have settled along the west coast of this long continent right from Alaska down to Peru."

HINDUS IN MODERN CANADA

Whether or not the Hindus of ancient India were the first colonizers of the Americas cannot be said with absolute certainty, and is a matter of debate among historians. The modern history of immigration from India to Canada commenced in 1903 when five men from the Punjab state in India landed in Vancouver, and another five in Victoria, British Columbia. They were farmers or retired soldiers with no education, and they all settled in British Columbia. Although a large majority of them were Sikhs, they were all called "Hindus" in Canada. These Punjabi pioneers had a common cultural and religious background as Sikhism in India is considered a stream flowing from Hinduism. In Punjab, Hindus and Sikhs are completely intertwined- socially, culturally and religiously. In British Columbia too, they lived as one community and struggled together to create a place for themselves in Canadian society. Although the history of Hindus and Sikhs in Canada is inseparable, the focus of this chapter is on primarily on early Hindu immigrants.

DEVICHAND, THE FIRST HINDU IMMIGRANT

Among the earliest group of immigrants from India was a Hindu Brahmin called Devichand. He was an enterprising and educated man, and claimed to be a friend of the Maharaja of Nabha, a princely state in Punjab. After living in Victoria for some time, he moved to Vancouver. In 1905, he established an employment agency and brought small groups of immigrants from India to work in unskilled and manual jobs in British Columbia. Their number gradually increased to 432 by 1906 although not all of them were brought in by Devichand. Although small in number, they were highly visible on account of their skin colour and unique attire. Still, Nobody took much notice of them except Thomas McGuigan, the Vancouver City Clerk who was irked by their presence. He started writing angry letters to the Federal Superintendent of immigration. Initially, his protest was ignored by the senior officials of the immigration department, but he started drawing media attention, and the Canadian government gave in to the pressure. A Royal Commission, headed by MacKenzie King, then deputy Minister of Labour, was appointed to investigate the sudden influx of immigrants from India. It is hard to believe that such a small number of immigrants would become a national issue, especially when they had arrived in Canada legally. Since India was a part of the British Empire, its people were considered British citizens and had the legal right to come to Canada just as much as the Australians and New Zealanders. But this legal fact was irrelevant to Canadians who wanted to keep Canada a White Man's country.

DEVICHAND, A SCAPEGOAT

The Royal Commission's report concluded that the migration of Hindus to Canada was not spontaneous; it was a well organized scheme. It outlined three main reasons for the sudden influx of immigrants from India during the period 1904 to 1906:

1. To promote their business, the commission agents for some shipping companies were prompting people in India and other British colonies to migrate to Canada.

1. Pamphlets were being distributed in the rural areas of Punjab and Bengal urging people to take advantage of the economic opportunities in the U.S.A. and Canada, particularly in British Columbia.-

3. Devichand and some other individuals were making money by luring people to emigrate to Canada for a better life. They were entering into verbal agreements to find them employment and facilitating their settlement.

Since none of these activities were illegal, although they were called "unpatriotic to the Empire" by Mackenzie King, nothing could be done at the political level to stop Hindus from entering Canada. However, something had to be done to satisfy the people like McGuigan, and a scapegoat had to be found. Devichand's presence in Vancouver proved useful to some crafty civil servant. When some immigrants refused to pay Devichand for his services after their arrival in Canada, he threatened to have them deported, and used other pressure tactics to recover his fees. Devichand was arrested and charged with 'obtaining money under false pretences'. It is reported that Devichand was so rich that to secure his release, he had paid for his bail in sovereign gold coins. His case was heard on July 18th, 1906, and attracted a lot of media attention. It was alleged that his operation was quite extensive as he had brought 52 workers to Canada in one ship alone. He was acquitted and reported to have boasted that he wanted to replace Chinese and Japanese workers with his own countrymen. The *Daily Province* stated that Devichand had said:

"In the coming struggle, the Hindus will win hands down. My countrymen are skilled, and on this account it pays the employers to give them the higher wages than those earned by the other Asians. The local saw millers have assured me that they can give employment to 2000 of my countrymen. They are needed in lumber camps and sawmills. I am negotiating with parties in India with a view to drawing attention to the grand opportunity which awaits the sober and industrious Hindus in Canada."

Devichand's 'crusade' came to a halt when he returned to India in July, 1907, a year after his trial, with his wife and child. Although he had said that he was going home for domestic reasons, it is quite possible that he may have been subjected to constant harassment and threats. Incidentally, his wife was the first and the only Indian woman in Canada at that time as Indian workers were not allowed to bring their families to Canada.

THE *PARIAHS* OF CANADA

The history of the early Indo-Canadian pioneers, is written with sweat and tears. They worked as railway line laborers, fruit pickers, laborers in logging camps, lumber yards and saw mills. They did back breaking hard labour for long hours in primitive and harsh working conditions. Their wages were lowest among all the immigrant workers, including the Chinese. At work, they had to endure the racial insults and overt hostility of white fellow workers who, in some instances, physically assaulted them. However, their employers admired them as hard working and loyal employees.

Socially, they were an island of *pariahs*, totally isolated from the mainstream society. Since British Columbians resented their presence and would not rent out their properties to them, they faced a very serious accommodation problem. They had to live in over crowded and squalid conditions in the slum areas of Vancouver. Some, unable to find accommodation, had to live in makeshift tents, and did their cooking on the pavement. They were not allowed to bring their wives and children to Canada and, therefore, several males shared a commune type of household. Each household was a self-sustained and cohesive unit, providing economic and psychological support to each member. They developed their own social welfare system. The sick and unemployed were looked after by the earning members of the household.

The Indo-Canadian pioneers were the victims of the most blatant and vicious form of racial discrimination in every aspect of life. Although small in numbers, they were considered as undesirable aliens and a threat to white Canada. They were humiliated, harassed and shunned by Canadians. Not only were they treated inhumanely, they also had to face legislated injustice and systemic discrimination at all levels of government.

"KEEP CANADA WHITE" CAMPAIGN

The departure of Devichand did not stop the steady flow of immigrants from India. In 1908, their population in Canada increased to 5,179 which the alarmed British Columbians called "Hindu Invasion". Very soon, the slogan *Keep Canada white* echoed the valleys of British Columbia. This was not the slogan of an ultra right wing racist group but what the people of British Columbia demanded, and the politicians at all levels of government heeded their call. The people, press and politicians joined hands to keep Canada white. The hostile agitation in B.C. against immigration from Asia started with the formation of the Asiatic Exclusion League headed by Herbart H. Stevens, the flamboyant Alderman of Vancouver city. He declared:

> "We contend that the destiny of Canada is best left in the hands of the Anglo-Saxon race, and are utterly and irrevocably opposed to any move which threatens in the slightest degree this position.....As far as Canada is concerned, it shall remain white, and our doors shall be closed to Hindus as well as other Orientals."

The *Keep Canada White* campaign was not a local affair limited to Vancouver. Sir Richard McBride, the Premier of B.C. as well as MacKenzie King, when he was a federal deputy minister of labour in 1908, also staunchly defended the concept of keeping Canada a white man's country on social, political and economic grounds. The major newspapers of Vancouver, *Daily Province* and *The Sun,* did their part to whip up the *Hindu Invasion* hysteria. The letter's to the editors, editorials and columns heaped insults on Indo-Canadians. "So the wily Hindu is invading your beautiful British Columbia? He is ignorant and most immoral", said one letter to the editor of *Daily Province* of the 29th December, 1906. This is what *The Sun* wrote about allowing their families to Canada:

> "The Hindus.....crowded in one room......the Hindu women and children should not be admitted.....the safety of the white women and children would eventually be placed in jeopardy through the increasing influx of Hindus who lived in immediate vicinity of their colony......and they lived in filth and squalor."
>
> (February 16th 1912)

> "......but there is the point of view of the white settler in this country who wishes to keep the country white with white standards of living and morality. The vast majority of the intelligent population will realize the danger to which British Columbia and more of Canada too, will be exposed if we permit the immigration of Hindus with their families into the Dominion.
>
> (June 17th 1913)

The Canadians who openly supported the Indo-Canadians were some church groups and private individuals. Outlined below are some samples of opinions of the Canadians who opposed the racist concept of *Keep Canada White* on ethical grounds. These statements are quoted in *People of India in North America*, the work of Dr. I. M. Muthanna, an Indo-Canadian scholar from Vancouver.

One Miss E. Lindsay of Toronto wrote to a newspaper in 1916:

> "So you have come to us, Eastern brothers, come with the words of your seers. If you have a message to give to the West, we will hear with open minds and hearts."

Another critic, E. Mannings, wrote to the *Daily News*

advertise

"As a city and country, we are writing history and we are writing a very ugly page now.......Our treatment of the Hindus is a disgrace to any civilized nation."

Indignant Wallace Wright pleaded with his fellow Canadians:

> "Are we not in Canada making ourselves rather ridiculous over what is called the 'Hindu question'? The Dominion has admitted many most undesirable Europeans, Galicians, Armenians Doukhobers etc. yet we are keeping out men of tried loyalty who have fought for our Empire in many climes and arduous campaigns"

Alas ! Such voices of reasoning and compassion fell on deaf ears.

THE LEGISLATED DISCRIMINATION

The Federal government gave in to the public pressure and enacted harsh legislation to ban immigration from Asia. One such legislative device was the 'Continuous Passage' rule of 1908. It required Indian immigrants to come to Canada only by continuous passage from India when there was no direct shipping service from India to Canada. To make the entry of people from India more difficult, the Order-in-council of the 9th May, 1910 also required that anyone of Indian origin must possess $200 at the time of entering Canada. As a result, immigration from India dried up by the end of 1912. Those who went to India for a short visit were not permitted to re-enter Canada. The wives and children of Indo-Canadians could not join them. These restrictions were not lifted until 1924 after B.C. Indo-Canadians waged a long and hard agitation that included costly court battles. Even these crafty legal hurdles did not deter Indians from coming to Canada.

To fight against legislated racial discrimination and the hate propaganda of newspapers and politicians, some educated Hindus and Sikhs formed the Hindustani Association with Bhag Singh as its President, and Gurudatt Kumar as the

General Secretary. Later on, they also made the struggle for the freedom of India as a part of their agenda. The Sikh Temple in Vancouver, built in 1907, became the hub of their activities. They lobbied hard, raised large sums of money for many court encounters with the federal department of immigration, and even had their own English language publications to educate the public of British Columbia. Amongst the most notable community leaders was Tarakanath Das from Bengal who first came to Vancouver and then moved to the U.S.A. in 1906 to study at the State University of Seattle. He started the well known *Free Hindustan* journal from Vancouver in May 1908. In the editorial of the first issue of the *Free Hindustan*, Das proclaimed:

> "The avowed object (of the journal) was preaching of the doctrine of political, social and religious freedom, and the initial number of the magazine was devoted largely to a consideration of the question of barring of Dominion immigration doors to Hindus."

The Indo-Canadian community became assertive and galvanized under the capable and sophisticated leadership of people like Tarakanath Das, Kapur Singh Sidhu, Mayo Singh Manhas and Gurudatt Kumar. In response to Herbart Stevens's hostile uttering against his countrymen, Gurudatt Kumar retaliated equally hard. The *Daily Province* of May 6th 1912 reported his response:

> "Let Mr. Stevens study the history of the British. Where were the people of Great Britain 2000 years ago ? The Anglo-Saxon race is nothing but a part of the Caucasian race which is the name of the Aryan race, and we the Hindus and Sikhs are proud to belong to such a race which was highly civilized when the people of Britain and Europe were mere savages."

THE 'KAMAGATA MARU AFFAIR'

The history of Indo-Canadians pioneers would be incomplete without mentioning the so called 'Kamagata Maru affair'. In April 1914, 367 Indians, mostly Sikhs, reached the shores of Vancouver in a Japanese ship called *Kamagata Maru* chartered by a Gurdit Singh, an Indian entrepreneur. They had a hostile reception from the British Columbians who demanded that the ship must be turned back. They were not allowed to disembark, even though they had satisfied all legal requirements for immigration to Canada. The ship sat in the Vancouver harbor for three months while the Indo-Canadian community of Vancouver fought a very costly legal battle against the department of immigration. The passengers were treated worse than prisoners, and were forced to live under the most inhumane conditions. The immigration officers refused to have the garbage removed from the ship, and cut off the water and food supply. Many passengers became ill and one died. When the Indo-Canadians lost their case in the highest court of Canada and all lobbying efforts failed, the ship was forcibly pushed out of the harbor by a navy barge while a huge crowd jeered and taunted the passengers. The Indo-Canadians consider the *Kamagata Maru Affair* as the most blatant and despicable act of racism, and the darkest episode in the history of Canada.

THE ECONOMIC BASE ESTABLISHED

The hardships the early pioneers underwent made them a cohesive and resilient community in British Columbia. With immense struggle and hard work, many of them accumulated sufficient capital and started their own businesses, saw mills and farms. The purchase of 441 acres of land on North Shore under the capable leadership of Teja Singh and Gurudatt Kumar, became a landmark of their economic prowess. The better educated younger generation entered skilled trades and professions. Gradually, the mainstream society recognized their entrepreneurial spirit and contribution to the economy, and discrimination became less severe. By 1930, it had become evident that Indo-Canadians had planted their roots firmly in the Canadian soil. However, politically, they were still treated as second class citizens. They were not allowed to vote in the elections for any of the three levels of government.

In October 1910, Gurudatt Kumar unsuccessfully challenged the ban on Asians' right to vote in the civic elections of Vancouver City.

THE STRUGGLE FOR POLITICAL RIGHTS

Having established a sound economic base, the Indo-Canadian community in B.C. mounted a very sophisticated campaign to acquire the right to vote. The suffrage movement, spearheaded by prominent Hindu and Sikh leaders, remained a burning issue until the 1940's. Many highly educated Hindus from California visited Canada regularly to lend their active support to this campaign. Amongst such helpers was Dr. Tarakanath Das from California. The emergence of the B.C. Co-operative Commonwealth Federation (CCF) party gave a new impetus to the suffrage movement. The CCF party staunchly supported the Indo-Canadians' demand for political equality. When the CCF brought up this issue in the provincial legislature, the hostility towards Indo-Canadians reached a new height. The provincial Labour Minister, G.S. Pearson commented:

" The Hindu is not helping us to maintain the standard of living we have set up in the province. There is nobody in the province as unreliable. dishonest and deceitful as the Hindu. They break every regulation we have......we are justified in excluding them from the full rights of citizenship."

Many prominent visitors and diplomats from India also helped the suffrage movement. In 1945, India appointed M.R. Ahuja as its first Trade commissioner to Canada. The appointment of Ahuja, based in Toronto, resulted from Canada's desire to expand its trade with India. Ahuja strongly expressed his displeasure over the shabby treatment of Indo-Canadians in B.C. In 1946, a prominent Hindu from India, P. Konanda Rao of the influential Servants of India Society, came to Montreal to attend a conference on international migration. Rao was very much distressed by the second class status of his countrymen, and highlighted the vote issue. After attending the conference, he went on a Canada wide speaking tour to arouse public opinion against racial discrimination.

Another Hindu human rights activist from India who played a very crucial role in the movement was D.P. Pandia. It is believed that Pandia was a lawyer and a private secretary to Mahatma Gandhi, and had first come to the United States to lobby the US Congress to grant the status of naturalized citizenship to 3000 Indians who had settled in the US prior to 1924. He first came to Canada in 1939 to deliver a lecture to the Theosophical Society of Canada. At that time, he accompanied B.C. Indo-Canadian leaders to Ottawa to present their case to allow a small number of illegal immigrants to stay in Canada. In 1946, he returned to Canada to assist the Vote Movement and met with the B.C. Elections Act Committee. Finally, on April 2, 1947, the B.C. legislature restored the right to vote to all Asians. However, they were still denied the right to vote in the federal and civic elections.

As India became independent in 1947, the denial of the voting right to Indo-Canadians in federal elections had become a political embarrassment to the Canadian government. When Canada became involved in the formation of the United Nations, the refusal to extend basic political rights to Indo-Canadians directly contradicted the UN Charter of Rights. Canada's desire to acquire trading privileges with independent India also played a crucial role in softening the Canadian government's attitude on this issue. Following the change in the B.C. legislature, the Canadian Parliament also passed legislation allowing all Asians to vote in the federal elections.

The Indo-Canadian community then shifted its attention to the municipal legislation which still barred them from voting in the local elections. In the fall of 1947, the Cities of Vancouver and Victoria enacted legislation to give them the voting rights. In spite of these victories, the Indo-Canadians' struggle against legislated injustice and inequality still continued against the discriminatory immigration policy of the federal government.

6.

A PROFILE OF HINDU CANADIANS

THE NEW PIONEERS

Although the overtly discriminitive legislation was removed, gradually, the flow of new immigrants from the Indian sub-continent was reduced to a trickle as a result of tight administrative controls and the quota system imposed by the government of Canada. According to the *Census Canada, 1961*, the population of South Asians (from India, Pakistan, Sri Lanka) in Canada was 6,771 of which 4,526 lived in British Columbia. During the late fifties and early sixties, only a handful of Hindu professionals, mostly teachers and engineers, arrived in Ontario and British Columbia. The major influx of Hindus did not commence until after 1967 when the immigration policy of Canada was made non-discriminatory and global. A large majority of these new pioneers settled in Ontario. According to *Census Canada* 1986, there were 300,000 Hindus in Canada of which about one-third lived in Metropolitan Toronto. This was the first time that the Canadian population was classified by religion.

THE MIDDLE CLASS URBANITE HINDUS

As a result of media sensationalism, many Canadians have the misconception that the immigrants from India are poor and running away from starvation and disease. Such a stereotype has been created by the Canadian media's portrayal of India as a sea of human misery. This one-sided and negative presentation about India has prevented Canadians from discovering the phenomenal economic progress India has achieved since it became independent in 1947. The massive industrialization in India has produced a rapidly growing urban middle class. Since the poor Indians have neither financial resources nor skills or education, they cannot emigrate to Canada. Since the wealthy Indians have no desire to leave, most Indian immigrants are from the newly emerged educated middle class from the major urban centres of India.

Among all the sub-groups from India, Hindus are the best educated new Canadians. They do not conform to the stereotyp of the early Indian pioneers. Prior to migrating to Canada, most Hindu Canadians lived comfortably, if not affluently, in India and owned properties and businesses. Most of them were professionals, para-professionals or white collar workers. According to *Census Canada 1986*, 50 % of immigrants from India were professional and technocrats, and were much better educated than the Canadians of British origins. For example, 51 % of immigrants from India were university graduates compared to 17 % from Britain. Also, 78 % of immigrants from India had high school education compared to 66 % from Britain. Considering their urban middle class background, logically, these figures would be much higher for Hindu Canadians.

This new breed of Hindu Canadians is playing an important role in every aspect of economic life in their newly adopted country. There are Hindu medical doctors, scientists, university professors, engineers, accountants, senior civil servants, managers, technologists, prosperous business owners and office workers. It would be hard to find many illiterate or unskilled Hindu Canadians except some senior citizens who came to join their adult chidren. However, many educated Hindus who cannot find a job in their own field of work are forced to accept lower paid, entry level jobs. Many doctors, engineers or accountants have to accept work as parking lot attendants, security guards and factory workers.

THE MULTICULTURAL HINDUS

Like Canada, India is a multi-cultural and multi-religious mosaic. What has been happening in Canada during the last century, happened in India over a period of five thousand years. People of many races, religions and cultures came to settle in India from foreign lands; their social and cultural interaction produced a multi-racial society. Basically, there are three major racial groups in India: fair skinned Çaucasians, Mongoloid and the dark ancient Dravidians. These three races have merged and mingled to the extent that it is impossible to describe Hindus' racial identity. The skin colours among Hindus range from Nordic fairness in the North to Nubian blackness in the South. In the East, oriental facial features predominate while Caucasian looks are more dominant in the North-Western regions. A whole range of racial and colour combinations and variations is present in Hindu Canadians.

Although Hindus in Canada come from various regions of India, speaking over a dozen different languages, there are four major linguistic groups that are dominant: Gujaratis from North-West, Bengalis from the East, Punjabis from the North and Tamils from the South. The other smaller groups are Sindhis, Kashmiris, Malayalis, Kannads, Biharis, Maharashtrians and the people from the Uttar Pradesh. Each of these sub-groups has its own organization for cultural and religious activities. But they also jointly participate in numerous secular Indian associations in each province of Canada. It is interesting to note that they use English as a link language to communicate with each other.

Apart from India, there are Hindus in Canada who come from other countries, mostly British colonies, to which their ancestors had migrated from India a few generations ago. Notably among them are from South and East Africa, Trinidad, Guyana, Fiji, Marutius and Malayasia. Many of these groups lost contact with India and produced a *'hybrid'* Hindu culture as a result of interaction with other races and cultures of their newly adopted lands. Most of these Hindus only speak English and have their own cultural and religious organizations.

NO RESIDENTIAL GHETTOS

Based on their experience with some immigrant groups, many Canadians fear that immigrants from India will decrease the property value in their neighborhood by establishing an ethnic ghetto. This notion is totally false in the case of Hindus from India. Since they mostly come from major urban centres in India, speak English and do not feel socially insecure, they do not create ghettos by living with their own kinds. Usually, Hindus buy houses in middle class to expensive residential areas. They feel quite at ease in both ethnic and mainstream neighborhoods.

SMALL FAMILY UNIT

There is a body of opinion in Canada that immigrants from India have large families and will 'swamp' Canada. Again, this misconception stems from the poor image they have of India. To an average Canadian, India and overpopulation seem inseparable themes. They are not aware that educated urbanite Hindus in India do not produce large families whether they emigrate to Canada or not. Since Hindu Canadians have a middle class urban background, a typical Hindu family in Canada has usually two or three children. Many prosperous Hindu businessmen and professionals also have a maid living in their household. One will rarely see uncles, aunts or cousins living under the same roof. Even in urban India, the traditional joint family system is being discarded by educated middle class people. However, a few Hindus may have their old parents living with them as an economic necessity; some affluent Hindus establish a separate home for their retired parents from India. In any event, it is very uncommon to find more than 4 or 5 people living in a typical Canadian Hindu household.

FAMILY UNITY AND HARMONY

The traditional Hindu value system emphasizes family unity and harmony. Here is such a prescription as found in

Hindu scriptures:

"O family members! May you live together amicably and as equals for the sake of your common goals like the spokes of a wheel which are all equal and converge at the core. Do not cause conflicts amongst you and separate. By talking with civility and showing respect for one another, by rendering assistance to one another and having tender, warm feelings for one another, proceed along the road of prosperity."

Atharva Veda iii.30.5

In a Hindu society, familial obligations are very important. A Hindu child's duties to his family over-ride all other relationships. Family relationships are considered to be more important than the peer-group relationships. Hindu Canadians usually complain that the mainstream culture overemphasizes rights and pays very little attention to responsibilities. Hindu parents in Canada expect conformity to their important cultural values and traditions, while mainstream society emphasizes the bond of their peers. This conflict becomes an extra source of stress both to parents and children. However, after an initial period of adjustments and compromises on the part of both parents and children, the latter begin to appreciate many positive aspects of their Hindu heritage. The children feel that living in two worlds makes their lives richer and much more interesting than those of their mainstream peers. Hindu children believe they have the best of both worlds.

In an average Hindu Canadian family, the parent-child relationship is very close. The parents' lives revolve around building their children's careers and futures. Since the incident of marriage breakdown and domestic conflict, compared with the mainstream society, is extremely low, a Hindu child usually grows up in a peaceful and stable family environment. As a result, juvenile deliquency problems are very uncommon. The child enjoys the warmth of the security blanket, both psychological and economical, provided by this closeness. Some children complain that their parents' excessive attention and protective behavior stifles them. Many Hindu children lack life skills because they are too dependent on their parents.

Most children live with their family until they finish their education and get married. Some would stay with their family even after they are married, in order to accumulate enough money to buy their own house. In most cases, parents also financially assist them in purchasing a house. Generally, parents do not put any pressure on their adult children to leave home. When they do leave the family, the emotional trauma for Hindu parents is usually a lot more severe than for the mainstream parents. Even after marriage, the close family ties are still maintained.

SPECIAL EMPHASIS ON EDUCATION

Hindus in India have always revered learned men and women above all others. Higher learning is preferred over acquiring wealth as a means to gain respect and recognition in the society. Education is considered the greatest investment and security that no one can take away. It is the most effective way to prove one's worth. This tradition is still practised by most Hindu Canadians. They are quite willing to undergo any amount of economic hardship and make personal sacrifices in order to give a university education to their children. They believe that paying for the children's education is the parents' responsibility as well as a sacred duty. Therefore, their children do not have to worry about part-time or summer jobs and government loans in order to finance their educational needs. In fact, most parents discourage their children from working part-time during the school year as it may adversely affect their academic performance.

Hindu parents push their children to study hard, and closely monitor their performance at school. Usually, they are not satisfied if their children achieve only average marks. School drop-outs are infrequent. To drop out of school brings shame to the entire family; higher academic achievement is a source of pride. Many Hindus in Canada are of the opinion that they must follow the Jewish model in order to overcome racial prejudice. Therefore, they put tremendous pressure on their children to acquire university education. Along with Orientals, Hindu students are gaining recognition for their intellectual prowess. A very large number of them are encouraged by their parents to choose such prefessions as medicine, dentistry, engineering, pharmacology, computer science, law, accountancy, business management, teaching and research; not many choose a career in blue collar trades.-

PEACEFUL & NON-VIOLENT PEOPLE

Non-violence is an important component of the Hindu way of life. Hindus consider physical violence a human weakness; forgiveness is a strength in human character. Hindu Canadians counsel their children to refrain from physical violence. In the event of a confrontation at school, they advise their children to use verbal skills, tacts or withdrawal in response to a physical challenge. Generally speaking, Hindu students are much less physically aggressive than other students. However, many Hindus feel that the school authorities usually do nothing or very little to combat racially motivated harrassment and violence in schools. Out of fear for the safety of their children, many parents enrol them in martial art courses in order to meet the challenge of racial harrassement. They consider this approach as a practical one.

It would not be an overstatement to say that the crime rate in Hindu communities in Canada is extremely low. They respect and admire the police and the justice system in Canada. They live with peace and harmony in their adopted land. It is also noteworthy that Hindus do not import to Canada the political problems of India (despite extreme provocations, sometimes, from other religious groups) nor do Hindus in India export political or sectarian violence to foreign lands.

DATING & SEXUAL BEHAVIOR

According to Hindu social norms, a sexual relationship is reserved exclusively for married life. Therefore, pre-marital and extra-marital sex is abhored, and common-law relationships are totally unacceptable. Dating for the purpose of sexual experimentation is considered morally degradating and therefore frowned upon. A courting young Hindu couple do not face the dilemma of whether or not to 'go all the way' on the first date; what they worry about is whether or not it would be proper to 'go all the way' on the wedding night.

Hindu Canadians admire and adopt many aspects of the mainstream culture, but the sexual behavior of young Canadians is not one of them. They are often shocked and horrified by the sexual promiscuity among young Canadians. They are very disturbed by current social trends: an alarmimgly high rate of teenage pregnancies; condom dispensing machines in schools; virginity or celibacy as a social stigma; unwed motherhood is acceptable; TV sitcom shows like *'Married with Children'* are popular; movies with raunchy sex scenes and obscene language are shown on TV during family hours; and smut peddling is called freedom of expression. Hindu Canadians feel that these are not the signs of an advanced culture, but a morally decaying society. They attribute this moral degeneration to the fact that religion in North American society is no longer an integral part of human development, and traditional morality is shunned in the name of individual freedom or not taught in schools or families. Hindus are well aware that their traditional values are generally considered as social backwardness by their Canadian peers, but they are very proud of their 'backwardness' which they try hard to instil in their children.

Hindu Canadians do want their children to become fully integrated into the mainstream society, but they are extremely worried about the moral standards and sexual behavior of their Canadian born children. They strongly urge them not to emulate the sexual behavior of their peers. They watch the behavior of their children like hawks, and teach them some techniques to fight off the peer pressure. The issue of dating has become a source of conflict in many Hindu families. The parents' vigilence and over-protectiveness causes a great deal of stress and frustration for the children, as they have to juggle the peer-pressure with the parent-pressure. Some young Hindus give in to the peer pressure but keep their social life a well-guarded secret from their parents. However, a large majority of Hindu youths do accept their parents' traditional values. The scare of AIDS and other sexually transmitable diseases give them a strong reason to follow their parents' advice. On the whole, it would not be totally wrong to say that the pattern of the sexual behavior of Hindu youths is not exactly the same as that of their mainstream peers. Although parenting becomes extremely challenging to Hindu parents, they do have some success in instilling their children with traditional values. By doing so, they also inject a healthy dose of badly needed traditional values into the bloodstream of Canadian society.

THE DEMOLITION OF CASTE BARRIERS

Most Canadian Hindus belong to three upper castes, but some educated Shudras, by virtue of their education and skills, have also emigrated. In relation to casteism, what has happened in the Hindus community in Canada is nothing short of a social revolution. In a relatively short period of time, they have totally shed their caste consciousness- something which social reformers in India could not achieve over the centuries. When Canadian Hindus socially interact, unlike in India, they do not even think about enquiring into each other's caste background. Usually, the new Hindu Canadians socialize within their own linguistic or professional groups, and the caste is not a barrier to friendship. Among professional Hindus, even language is an irrelevant factor in forming a social circle. One does not come across many formal, social or cultural, associations organized purely on the basis of caste.

Inter-caste marriages are common among Canadian Hindus. Not many Hindu parents insist that their Canadian born children marry within their own caste. Personal merits are more important than one's caste. In some cases, however, linguistic considerations may be stronger than caste as some parents prefer that their children marry in a Hindu family who speaks the same regional Indian language, e.g. Bengali, Hindi, Marathi or Gujarati etc. But, Canadian born young Hindus who choose their own life-partners rarely heed such advice. In some instances, Brahmins, Kshatriyas and Vaishyas have married Shudras without much fuss. In India, such matrimonial alliances still alienate the upper caste parents even in the modern urbanite Hindu society.

This social revolution came about without starting an anti-caste movement in Canada. It did not require any zealous social reformer's crusade to eradicate casteism. There are many factors that together demolished the caste barriers so rapidly. First and foremost, modern Hindus are the product of a British system of education, and came with a prior knowledge of the Western society and its values. Secondly, a large majority of Hindu immigrants are well educated and come from a modern and urban background in India. The caste system in urban India is disintegrating much more rapidly than in villages. Therefore, Hindu Canadians tend to be liberal and open-minded, and predisposed to crossing the caste barriers. Thirdly, when they first came to Canada, the Hindu population was so small that it was impossible to form a social circle within their own caste. The inter-caste social interaction destroyed the centuries old prejudices and pre-conceived notions about each other. Lastly, Hindu parents did not transfer their caste based prejudices to their Canadian born children, knowing full well that the latter would not practise casteism anyway.

SOCIAL INTEGRATION

Since Hindus themselves are a culturally diversed group, Canadian multi-culturalism is not anything new to them. They are much better equipped to live in multi-cultural Canada than the immigrants who were culturally homogeneous in their old country. However, despite the high level of education and their urban background, Hindus do feel a cultural shock when they first arrive in Canada, although much less than many other groups of cultural origin, including many Europeans. One must not forget that the British presence in India, which lasted for two centuries, did have a profound impact on Indian culture, especially in major urban centres. Urban Indians are educated under the British system of education, and have inherited many British institutions, customs and traditions. Educated Hindu urbunites in India often emulate the Western lifestyle. Along with Hindi, English is still a national language used in higher education, business and administration. With prior knowledge of English language and experience in Western culture, educated Hindu Canadians integrate into the mainstream society much faster than many other immigrant groups.

The second generation Hindus are often culturally indistinguishable from the mainsteam Canadians. Hindu parents encourage their children to mix freely with everybody at school and not to form a separate clique. In fact, many Hindu parents are worried that their Canadian born children will lose their cultural identity because of their own complacency in teaching them Hindu customs and traditions. Out of this fear, some Hindu parents have started sending their children to India during the summer break for cultural immersion. However, many parents complain that the new generation of urban and modern India is blindly imitating the North American pop culture and, therefore, sending their children to India for cultural orientation is of no value. These developments seem to indicate that the second generation Hindu Canadians may not remain a cultural minority, except for their colour, much to the chagrin of the first generation, unless immigration from India continues.

Hindu Canadians may not be the salt of the earth but they do make many painful and difficult adjustments in their personal lives and compromise many centuries of old traditions in order to become acceptable to the host society. Having read this observation, some 'multi-culturalism critics at large' are bound to ask, "but what about the Sarees and the dot on the Hindu women's forehead." This question merits an answer.

Firstly, neither Saree nor the red dot on the forehead is a religious requirement. Saree is not just a long dress; it is a six yard long piece of cloth with no seams at all, and gracefully wrapped. A red dot on the forehead declares them to be happily married, but there is also a spiritual significance explained elsewhere. Also, only a very small percentage of

Hindu women wear a Saree at work or in public places but as they have become highly visible it gives the impression that all Hindu women wear saree and red dots on the forehead primarily to flaunt their culture. After they have been in Canada for a few years, they limit the use of Saree and red dot to special cultural and religious events. To those few who prefer to wear a Saree all the time, it is simply a personal choice in the matter of fashion; they are not making a statement. They wear it because they like it. Moreover, traditional Indian dresses and jewellery are being copied by many fashion Gurus and have been introduced to Canadians as new fashion, although Canadian women may not be aware of this fact; nose ring or stud, anklets, cummerbund and baggy harem pants are just a few examples of this fashion plagiarism. A Saree could be considered another fashion trend- an authentic and original one. Lastly, one can argue that if a Sikh can wear a turban and Kirpan, a Jew can wear a skull-cap , (not to mention the very strange hair styles young Canadians have) wearing the graceful Saree as a dress and a red dot on the forehead as a facial make-up is not such a weird trend. After all, multicultural Canada is a reality, whether one accepts it or not.

POLITICAL INTEGRATION

India is the largest parliamentary democracy in the world. Therefore, Hindu Canadians are not strangers to the Canadian system of government. They are gradually appearing on the Canadian political scene. An increasing number of Hindus are becoming active in all three political parties. However, it would be fair to say that a large majority of them are affiliated with the Liberal Party, both at federal and provincial level. Recently, some Hindu businessmen and professionals have become active in the two other political parties. No Hindu has yet been elected to parliament or a provincial legislature, but many have contested party nominations and some have been candidates in the elections. Generally, they do participate in the election process enthusiastically.

Some people are surprized to learn that Hindu Canadians

do not have a political lobby or pressure group. There are many Hindu human rights activists, but they do not use their religious institutions as a forum for their struggle against racial prejudice. Generally, Hindus do not mix religion and politics, even though some Hindus view it as a weakness. Moreover, they also believe that the problems they face as a visible minority are not any different from those of the Sikhs, Moslems or Christians from the Indian Sub-continent. It does make more sense to them to join secular organizations that are fighting racism or sharing common goals.

7.

STATUS OF WOMEN

Those who believe that equality for women is a Western concept will be surprised to learn that ancient Hindus accorded women a place of equality, honour and dignity. In the Vedic society, women had the freedom to educate themselves, study the Scriptures and achieve the status of sages, saints and scholars. Hindu literature of ancient India features many women who excelled in intellectual endeavors. Among the most prominent female scholars who gave in-depth discourses on Vedas were Lopamudra, Urvashi, Yami, and Ghosha. The two most illustrious female scholars of Upanishadic age, Gargi and Maitreyi, had challenged and resoundingly defeated the Vedic genius Yajnavalkya in a theological debate in the court of King Janaka. These and many other episodes shatter the myth that Hinduism relegates woman to a inferior status or being subservient to man.

WOMAN, THE GODDESS

Hindus were the first to conceive God both in male and female form. Hindu Scriptures extol the worship of God as divine mother. Goddess, the Divine Mother, besides giving birth, also gives to Her children all the good things in life; Goddess Luxmi gives wealth and prosperity, Goddess Saraswati bestows knowledge and fine arts, and Goddess Durga provides protection. Therefore, the relationship between the human beings and God is compared with that of a child and a mother who gives birth to a child, nurtures him, gives him iife skills and showers him with love and tender care. It is because of this perfect analogy that Hinduism gives the mother a higher status than that of the father and teacher. According to Manu, the first Hindu law-maker of ancient India:

"The rank of a principal is equal to ten ordinary teachers, the rank of a father is equal to that of hundred principals. The rank of a mother is equal to that of one thousand fathers."

Manusmriti II. 145

WOMAN, THE BUILDER OF SOCIETY

Being the teacher of man, woman builds the foundation of society and shapes the destiny of the nation. Since the future of a nation depends upon the quality of the children it produces, motherhood occupies an exalted position in Hinduism. It is solely because of this reason that the role of a housewife is highly recommended for woman, although she does have the freedom to pursue any other occupation along with man. According to Hindu Scripture, Harit Smriti, " There are two categories of women; those who study the Vedas and the other scriptures and opt to pursue a philosophical path and those who, when they come of age, marry and become householders." In other words, a woman can either have a full-time career or be a full-time mother, but not both at the same time.

Being a housewife, according to traditional Hindu values, is not considered an inferior status for a woman. Many Hindus feel that the people in the West have difficulty comprehending this concept. That is why, they argue, when the Western world came into contact with India, they failed to understand or appreciate the Hindu attitude in respect of women; they erroneously formed the opinion that Hinduism considers woman as inferior to man.

Hindus who follow traditional family systems believe that the high quality of family life, conducive to bringing up virtuous children, cannot be maintained with part-time motherhood; the task of rearing children is too crucial to be entrusted to baby-sitters or nannies. Many Hindus hold part-time motherhood responsible for the lack of discipline in children, the decay in morality and other social problems of the younger generation.

A WOMAN'S STATUS IN A HINDU FAMILY

Hindus refer to an unmarried girl as a *Kanya*, meaning *radiant, illustrious, brilliant*, and this implies that a girl must acquire all such qualities that can make her excel in every field of activity. During the stage of girlhood, she must develop herself physically, mentally and spiritually in order to enter the life of a householder, the Grahasth Ashram.

According to Hinduism, the role of a woman in the household is equal to that of a man. The husband is called *Pati*, the protector and provider. The wife is called *Patni,* meaning the preserver and nourisher. Automatically, the division of labour is set out in the family. The Husband and wife team is compared to the two wheels of a chariot working in unison. Hinduism calls wife an *Ardhangini,* that is, *one-half of the whole.* The Hindu Scriptures state that no religious ceremony in a family is of any value unless both husband and wife participate in it sitting together. A wife is considered as manager and in-charge of the household, not just someone who cooks, cleans and makes babies. This is how a Hindu woman of Vedic age in India speaks of herself:

"I possess intellect. I have attained a high position in the family. I am a simple but intense individual who speaks truthfully and directly. I am capable of overcoming all difficulties and solving all problems. May my husband, favorably inclined towards me, abide by the rites and duties."

Rig Veda X. 159. 2

The Manusmriti, the first Hindu Code of behavior, outlined detailed rules for respecting women:

1. A lady who is the wife of another and is not a relative, should be addressed as Devi (Revered lady) or Bahen (Sister).

2. Sister-in-law, maternal aunt, paternal aunt, mother-in-law, and teacher's wife are all worthy of reverence. One should rise and greet them.

3. The paternal aunt, maternal aunt and elder sister should be treated as the mother.

4. The ladies of the house should always be honoured by the father, brother, husband and brother-in-law. Their esteem should be enhanced with gifts of clothing and jewellery which is for the welfare of the family.

5. Divinity resides in families in which the women are respected; where they are not, there is ruin.

6. There is rapid destruction of those families in which womenfolk suffer; where womenfolk have no difficulties that family always prospers.

7. Where insulted, women curse the household and that family is destroyed as if killed by various types of poison.

8. Those who seek blessedness for their families should liberally present adornment, clothing and foodstuff to the womenfolk on festivals and auspicious occasions.

9. That family is certainly blessed where there is mutual satisfaction and co-operation between husband and wife.

10. When the women in the family are happy the whole family is happy. The unhappiness of women results in the unhappiness of the whole family

STATUS DEVALUED

Although the woman of ancient India enjoyed equal rights with man, her status gradually declined as the Hindu society decayed over the centuries. Some Hindus would rather say that Hindu society decayed because of the decline in the woman's status, and thus the prophecy of Vedas came true. The glorious ancient India impoverished as woman, once considered the builder, preserver and nourisher of society was turned by man into a dependent whose role was to produce children and be subservient to her husband's commands. How did that happen ? Many explanations have been offered. Most importantly, her education was totally neglected after the Vedic period and, therefore, she was no longer equipped to play the important role that Vedas had assigned to her. Also, as Hindus moved away from the Vedic values, society became corrupt and no longer honoured woman. The man's control over both power and money corrupted him, and he subordinated woman, his other and equal half. Some Hindus also believe that the Islamic influence on India made woman inferior to man.

HINDU WOMEN OF MODERN INDIA

During the 18th and 19th century, several reform movements that swept across India emphasized that restoring to women the prestige they once enjoyed was the key to the betterment of the society in general. The work of the Arya Samaj, a reformative movement founded by Swami Dayananda in 1875, is most noteworthy in improving the condition of Hindu women. Arya Samaj established schools and colleges for girls and once again, like ancient India, women were allowed to serve as priests. The Western influence on India also made a positive contribution to the movement for emancipation of women, which continued until 1947 when India became independent. India has made tremendous strides in improving the status of women in less than fifty years. However, the progress of rural Hindu woman has been much slower as a result of the lower level of education in the rural population. In urban India, the progress made by women is absolutely phenomenal. In the institutions of higher learning, the modern Hindu women have equalled or surpassed the intellectual prowess of their Vedic contemporaries. They are entering in all professions once considered the exclusive bastion of male dominance. India has now women lawyers, judges, engineers, doctors, scientists and even pilots. In April 1992, Preety Sengupta claimed the honour of being the first Hindu woman to trek from the Canadian Artic to the Magnetic North Pole with an international team of men. In December 1992, the first batch of women recruits, mostly Hindus, joined the Indian Navy. In politics, Hindu women of India play a more prominent role than that of their Canadian counterparts. While Canada has yet to produce its first woman Prime Minister or Premier, the Late Mrs. Indira Gandhi (after Mrs

Bhandranayake of Sri Lanka) became the second female head of a government in the world, and an internationally acclaimed politician. India has elected more female politicians than the USA and Canada put together.

Among all the socio-psychological studies done in North America on educated women of modern India, the best known work is of M.L. Cormack of New York. In the forward of her book *The Hindu Women,* she states:

"Most of us have long carried around in our heads a confused picture- dingy and colorful at the same time- of the women of India. This picture is montage of scraps from various sources- the 'Mother India' notion of the 'downtrodden' women of India.....and the exotic sensuous women of the orient.....When I reached India in the fall of 1950 I was astonished to find something different from this montage: women of dignity, charm, simple beauty in all classes- farm women in the villages, middle class women in the cities, government women in New Delhi- women who were neither helpless and downtrodden nor absorbed in erotic gratification of pampered husbands........"

Whether or not the women of modern India are treated equally in family units is a question to which there is no simple or standard answer. The wife's status in a family unit depends on the socio-economic and educational level of the family. In the rural population with low level of education, the husband is still the bread winner in the family and the wife takes care of the household. She is expected to be subservient to her husband. The less educated working class families in the cities also follow the male dominated family system. Violence against women in this population is still a major social problem. The victims, usually uneducated and lacking in skills, suffer in silence due to economic dependence on their husbands, and the absence of government assistance. Moreover, the concept of a single woman living alone is not socially acceptable. Many community groups, usually run by upper-class and westernized women, have emerged to rescue the victims, but they are not very effective due to lack of resources. Their efforts, however, do raise the level of awareness of women's issues.

On the other hand, the urban middle and upper-middle class women have made tremendous progress in the post-independent India. They are well educated, emancipated and modern in outlook. In most young Indian families, as in Canada, both husband and wife have to hold jobs in order to maintain a good standard of living. The modern Hindu wife has to juggle her job and household duties, for doing domestic chores is still a taboo even for an educated husband. However, most working Hindu housewives in cities are luckier than their Canadian counterparts in easing the burden of housework. Since cheap labour is in abundance, hiring domestic help is a common practice. In many families, the parents living with their married son take care of their grand-children and the housework.

It should be mentioned here that the modern Hindu family is paying a heavy price for following the Western pattern of lifestyle. Part-time motherhood is severely straining the family fabric. The neglect of children due to working mothers is cloning the North American social problems in urban Hindu society. Drug abuse, school drop-outs, pre-marital sex and pregnancies, lack of respect for parents and elders, poor work ethics and other adolescent problems that exist among the children of liberated, modern working parents, have become a source of acute anxiety to Hindu community leaders in large cities. They are seriously questioning the wisdom of accepting the North American definition of gender equality. They wholeheartedly support the concept of equal opportunities for women, which is consistent with traditional Hindu values, but they have trouble accepting the notion that being a housewife is an inferior status for a woman. They believe that the primary purpose of education for a woman is not to prepare her for a job; a well educated mother nurturing virtuous children and sustaining a wholesome family life makes a far more superior contribution to society than bringing home a pay cheque; only women possess the innate qualities that are crucial for this role; managing a household is a highly skilled task; the idea of a husband going to work and a wife running the household is an equal division of labour i.e. the two equal and well-balance wheels of the chariot. The leaders of the Women's Lib movement in Canada may have trouble comprehending this Hindu concept of gender equality.

HINDU WOMEN IN CANADA

Since the large majority of Hindus come from the educated middle class of urban India, Hindu women in Canada are much better educated than any other religious group from South Asia. It would be very difficult to find a Hindu woman, with the exception of elderly women, with less than a high school education. However, their qualifications are lower than those of men. A large majority of them are working mothers. One will find Hindu women in almost every occupation ranging from university lecturers to industrial workers. Many highly qualified women are employed in clerical jobs either because their qualifications are not recognized in Canada or because of racial discrimination. Many employers would argue that the fault lies with the lack of job interview skills, and assertiveness, or effective oral communication due to shyness and a unique accent. For some women who lived a sheltered life in India and have never had to work, going for a job interview is a frightening experience. For the newly arrived Hindu woman, the cultural barrier makes it very hard to look straight into the eyes of a male prospective employer and to talk to him assertively to sell her skills. However, Canadian born women or the young urbanite women who were employed in India do not have those handicaps. Many Canadian Hindus believe that their girls are more studious and better academic performer than boys. They are able to balance the grace of a Hindu woman with the assertiveness of a North American woman.

On the domestic scene, Hindu women's problems are no different than those of Canadian working wives. Most Hindu women have to juggle their job and their domestic responsibilities. To Hindu men, the idea of doing domestic chores is a humiliating one, an assault on their male ego. However, most educated and sensible Hindu husbands gradually do learn to tame their ego and start sharing housework with their wives. However, they usually keep it as a well guarded secret from their friends. Many Hindus men complain that their wives have become too assertive, and it sometimes causes friction in their relationships. The incidence of physical violence against women do occur in Hindu homes, but at a much lower rate than in the mainstream families. Many victims usually suffer in silence due to the fear of breaking up the marriage. The social stigma of divorce still exists. Many Indian community groups, run by women, and Hindu organizations have recognized this problem and provide assistance to women in distress.

On the whole, Canadian Hindu women are much more liberated than the women in India. Their Sarees should not fool anyone ! Most Hindu temples and cultural organizations in Canada have women members on their management committees and boards. Some are even lay-priests and religious scholars. These developments are certainly revolutionary considering the fact that the bulk of Hindus came to Canada only during the last twenty-five years.

Scholar *Gargi* Debating With Vedic Genius *Yajnavalkya* In The Court Of King *Janaka* [ref. pg 71]

8.

THE HINDU MARRIAGE SYSTEM

There is no single or standard marriage system practiced by Hindus in Canada. Basically, there are three types of marriages:

1. Modified Arranged Marriages

2. North American Style Marriages

3. 'Compromised' or 'Middle Path' Marriages

1. Modified Arranged Marriages

Hindus consider marriage as a life long commitment and not a social contract. According to the traditional Hindu concept, marriage is a spiritual and unbreakable alliance which is not workable without the blessing and guidance of parents and elders. The choice of the mate is made entirely by the parents and elders in the family. The bride and the groom never even see each other before their wedding day. However, this practice is gradually being abandoned in modern urban India, and replaced by a modified version which allows the would-be bride and groom to approve each other. Let us examine the process in detail.

After completion of the education and finding a job, when a Hindu young man or woman is ready to start a family, the parents or elders ask their relatives and friends to search for a suitor. When a suitable candidate is found, the family elders begin a very discreet screening process through the extensive network of relatives and friends. Both families must belong to the same caste, religion and linguistic group. Hindus do not marry cousins or distant relatives with the same family name on either side of the parents, in order to avoid inbreeding. The suitor's likes and dislikes, nature, habits, interests, and temperament, are compared with those of the eligible bachelor's, to ensure that the two will be compatible. Equally important is the socio-economic and educational background of the candidate's family. Generally, if the covert investigation reveals a history of divorce, gambling, alcoholism, violence, dishonest behavior or some other socially unacceptable trait about the suitor or his or her family, the negotiations are aborted in a very discreet manner without offending anyone. If both families believe that it would be an ideal match, then the astrological charts are compared by the family priest on both sides to check the couple's compatibility for the future. If both families are satisfied, the man and the woman are allowed to meet only once to talk and approve of each other. If they don't like each other, the negotiations break down. This situation is handled in a very tactful and diplomatic manner in order to ensure that there are no hard feelings on either side. If the couple give their consent to their respective parents, the engagement ceremony and wedding plans are discussed by the two families. Although no courting is allowed, some daring couples may manage to meet each other a few more times before the wedding day, without their parents' knowledge or consent.

The modified arranged marriage system is still practised in some Hindu families in Canada, especially among those of very conservative background or whose children were born in India, and exposed to traditional Hindu practices before emigrating to Canada. The Hindu youths born and raised in Canada rarely accept this system.

2. NORTH AMERICAN STYLE MARRIAGES

There are very few Hindu Canadians who approve of the free North American style dating and marriage that does not allow any active and direct involvement of the parents in the mate selection process. In some families, if a child rejects the parents' traditions, they try to counsel and persuade the rebellious son or daughter to choose a Hindu life partner in order to receive their approval and blessings. They do not consider it an unreasonable expectation. After all, people of other religions expect the same from their children. Generally, most Hindu parents are successful in this effort when they are able to convince their young child that a inter-religious marriage would cause a conflict in their marriage and generate a serious identity crisis at a later stage in their life, especially among the children of a mixed marriage. Given the fact that in the North American society there are already many stresses on marriage, marrying someone outside your own religion, not to mention the burden of being rejected by families on both sides, can put an extra strain on the fragile institution of marriage. They often point out to their children that the alarmingly high rate of marriage breakdown, 30% in Canada and 40% in the USA, is the direct result of the free-style dating and marriage system with total disregard for traditional values.

Inter-religious marriages are not totally uncommon in Hindu communities in Canada. Such marriages do cause a tremendous amount of anguish and tension in the family, but most Hindu parents will accept a new non-Hindu son-in-law or daughter-in-law into their family, especially when the new member makes a sincere effort to win over his or her in-laws. In some cases, such acceptance is superficial and pretentious. Some Hindu parents never recover from the shock of a inter-religious marriage of their child; their relationship is totally severed and they live in painful anguish. To Hindu parents, their children's marriage is the most important event of their lives and one to which they eagerly look forward. When parents become mere guests or helpless spectators at their child's wedding of which they did not approve, they consider it a tragedy in their lives and too heavy a price to pay for choosing Canada as their new home.

It must be clarified that marrying a Sikh, Buddhist or a Jain of Indian origin is not viewed as a inter-religious marriage by Hindus; they do not consider the people of these three faiths outside the Hindu fold. On the other hand, Hindu parents become highly disturbed if their son or daughter selects a Muslim for a life partner. They find it very difficult to overcome the centuries old animosity towards Muslims; this is a product of some unpleasant historical events. Many Hindus who are not very religious can usually accommodate a Christian in their family fold with some adjustments, after the initial shock and rejection. They think of Christians as liberal minded people like themselves.

In any event. it is also noteworthy that a Hindu would seldom demand conversion to his or her own religion as a precondition to marrying a non-Hindu. In a mixed marriage, usually, a Hindu has no objection to his or her spouse following his or her own faith. Some Hindus would consider this liberal attitude as a weakness among Hindus while other view it as living proof of their tolerance towards the religion of others and also as an expression of a strong sense of security in their own religion.

3. THE 'COMPROMISED' OR MIDDLE PATH MARRIAGES

Most first generation Hindus in Canada realize that their Canadian born children do not favour the traditional arranged marriage system, or its modified version in which they do have the free right to accept or reject the would-be spouse selected by their parents' wisdom and experience of life. On the other hand, they cannot totally accept the mainstream Canadian system of marriage with free courting. They are not so much against the idea of pre-marital dating; it is that the sexual experimentation that goes with it that they find to be completely an affront to their traditional moral code of behavior. Although mainstream Canadians may find it very hard to believe, pre-marital celibacy is neither a religious fanaticism nor idealism, but a fact of life in a middle class Hindu family.

However, true to their reputation for being liberal minded, Hindus in Canada have found a middle path marriage system for their Canadian born children, a compromise between the two extremes or best of the both worlds. They do not object to their children freely socializing with non-Hindu members of the opposite sex as long as the relationship is a friendship, and involves no serious romance or sexual experimentation. If they have not already selected a Hindu mate acceptable to the parents when they are ready for marriage, the family elders willingly provide the match-making and referral service with the traditional built-in screening process. However, for the sake of their children, they have also put aside the centuries old rigid caste system, astrological considerations and strong regionalism of the old country. When a suitable Hindu match is found, the man and the woman are introduced to each other and allowed to date in the Canadian way until they are ready to make a firm commitment. The sole purpose of the courtship is to get to know each other in order to ensure compatibility in every way. The courting couple is strongly advised to save the sexual encounter for the wedding night. Once they give a nod of approval to their respective parents, both families meet to plan the wedding. If the courtship does not materialize into a marriage, the family elders and friends resume their referral service until a suitor is discovered.

WHY HINDU MARRIAGES ARE SO RESILIENT ?

For a Canadian, unfamiliar with the Hindu culture, it would be unthinkable, or even repulsive, to marry a total stranger or even someone you only met briefly. On the other hand, it is equally true that the arranged Hindu marriages, with or without the approval element, are extremely durable as evidenced by the exceptionally low rate of divorce among Hindu Canadians. Hindu Canadians often wonder why one out of every three marriages in Canada fail, despite the fact that a commitment materializes only after a lengthy and free style dating, pre-marital sex and, in many cases, common-law living. Hindus offer many explanations for the resiliency of their traditional marriage system.

A sacred bond

Most importantly, a Hindu is brought up with the profound notion that marriage is a union of two souls destined by divine will on the basis of their deeds (Karmas) in their previous lives. Therefore, they consider it as their sacred duty to preserve it. They take their wedding vows seriously. When their marriage becomes turbulent, they try very hard to save it instead of thinking of divorce as an easy exit.

Celibacy helps too

Pre-marital Celibacy in a large majority of Hindu youths is still a reality and not an impossible-to-achieve ideal. Therefore, in most cases, a newly wed couple has never been exposed to any sexual experience or an intense emotional intimacy with a member of the opposite sex. They have no choice othei than to accept each other as they are, and not what they should have been. They consider the honeymoon as the beginning of a new phase in their lives in which they will explore each other. Before considering the traditional Hindu marriage as imprisonment for life with no early parole, let us examine the impact of pre-marital sex or emotional intimacy in the free Western style marriages

Generally speaking, before selecting a prospective spouse, a young Canadian would indulge in romantic and sexual encounters with several members of the opposite gender. Before their wedding night, both would have already experienced numerous episodes of colorful flirtations, successes and memorable moments with persons other than the one they finally choose for a wedlock. Even with the final choice, they have already done all the exploration there was, during the dating process. Having tried so many flavors and delights before the marriage, the slightest setback or disappointment in the marital relationship can provoke, consciously or otherwise, the memory of or comparison with other satisfying intimacies in the past. This can create a tremendous pressure on both partners, and even wreck the marriage. A Hindu couple has no past experiences to compare with. Therefore, they tend to be satisfied with the relationship they have developed within the confines of the married life.

Love cultivated and nurtured

Hindus believe that when two people of compatible backgrounds make a lifelong commitment to each other, love can be cultivated and nurtured. Those who are not familiar with Hindu society may think that such a relationship is artificial, impossible or a forced love. This is not necessarily the case. The arousal of love between the two total strangers is not beyond the scope of human emotions. Take, for example, the love of a mother or a father for their child. From the moment the child is born, the fountain of love in their hearts begins to spring and goes higher and higher as the child grows, regardless of what a third party may think of the child's physical appearance or personal attributes. Brothers and sisters love each other even though they did not choose each other. This can also be said even about an adopted or a foster child. Thus, emergence or cultivation of love between two strange adults living together, willing to adjust and accommodate each other, is not an impossibility.

Strong support from parents

Regardless of the process a Hindu couple may use for selecting a life partner, usually, the parents of both spouses play a crucial role both before and after their marriage. Not many Hindu sons or daughters would say to their parents, " It is my life, my marriage, it is none of your business." In Hindu families (following traditional values), a marriage is not the union between two individuals, but between two families. This bond not only gives a psychological boost to the newly wed couple, it is also a reliable source of help and support during any marital crisis. Both families have a strong sense of commitment to make the marriage of their loved ones successful. Respective parents, who understand their children well, are better marriage counsellors than an unknown psychologist would be.

Hindus treat divorce as a social stigma. If a couple is divorced, the parents of each spouse feel humiliated. A divorce can have a far reaching ripple affect ou both sides of the family. A Hindu couple's divorce would also make it very difficult for their unmarried brothers and sisters, as well as their own children, to find a suitable life partner. The family with a divorced member is considered *'ainted*, and treated like a serious *genetic disease*. This may sound unfair, but Hindus believe that each individual is the product of his or her family values and environment. Also, this puts a tremendous pressure on both partners of the troubled marriage to find solutions rather than rush for a divorce, in order to avert social humiliation and disgrace for their respective families, who have a vested interest in saving the troubled marriage of any member of the clan.

Despite the numerous built-in safety devices in the traditional Hindu marriage system, the increasing incidence of marriage breakdown is a source of anxiety to Hindu Canadians. Although the rate of divorce among Hindus in Canada is only a small fraction of that in mainstream society, the rate of marital failures is likely to accelerate among second generation Hindu Canadians as they shun collectivism and adopt individualism, and as the traditional parental role in the lives of their adult children diminishes.

SOME MARRIAGE RELATED ISSUES

THE DOWRY CUSTOM

The custom of dowry in Hindu society is, probably, as old as the institution of marriage. Dowry is known as *Dahej*, a distorted version of the Sanskrit word *Dayad* meaning *a portion of parental wealth*. It simply refers to the gifts the parents willingly give to their daughter on her wedding day.

This custom also has its roots in the ancient Hindu property laws. Until recently, most Hindus practised the joint family system: parents, grandparents and uncles on the father's side living under the same roof. Upon the parents' death, the eldest son inherits their entire wealth, but he only acts as a trustee. He is required to utilize this wealth wisely and justly for the welfare of the whole family. Since the female members no longer live in the parental household, after they get married, and reside with their husband's extended family, the dowry system is a designed to give the daughters and sisters their share of the family wealth. Traditionally, the dowry consists of a modest amount of cash and simple gifts- basic furniture, utensils, bedding, blankets and other household items that are necessary for the newly wed couple.-44-In its initial form, the dowry is an excellent idea; a voluntary act reflecting fairness and the parents' love for their daughter. It was never mandatory for the parents to give a dowry, nor did the groom or his family ever demand it. As time went by, most parents gave dowries to their daughters as if they were compulsory, sometimes even far beyond their financial ability, in an effort to adhere to an old custom. Some egocentric parents started using the dowry as a means to show-off their wealth. Many parents could not afford it, but it became a matter of prestige, and they had to incur enormous debts in order to *keep up with the Jones.* Some greedy grooms and their families started demanding expensive dowries as a condition of the marriage. Gradually, this perfectly sensible custom became a distortion, a curse to Hindu society, and the ruin of poor families.

THE BRIDE BURNING— IN CITIES

In major urban centres of modern India, the dowry system animated violence against some women whose parents could not meet the demands and expectations of their greedy husbands or their families. Some greedy middle class parents began considering the financial sacrifices they had to make in order to educate their son as a form of *'investment'*. When their son became employed in a lucrative profession, such as doctor, dentist, engineer, manager, senior civil servant or businessman, the parents began viewing the dowry received in the son's marriage as *a return on their investment.* They would negotiate with a prospective bride's family as if they were making a business deal, and they demanded the dowry including a large amount of cash and other luxury goods- car, expensive furniture, domestic appliances, colour TV, VCR etc., and a grand reception in a five star hotel for the groom's wedding party. They would make a deal with the highest bidder for their son. After the wedding, if it so turned out that the bride's parents did not fully meet their demand or expectation, they would make their daughter-in-law's life very miserable by mistreating her. In many cases, the mental torture caused by constant taunting and goading by the in-laws would drive her to commit suicide. In some cases, they killed the daughter-in-law by setting her on fire and then claimed that she had committed suicide. The wealth hungry parents would then arrange a new marriage for their son and get an additional *return on their investment.*

The increasing number of such incidents of *bride burning,* heavily played by media, caused a public outcry against the evil of *dowry-on-demand.* Many social reformers started educational campaigns urging Hindus to give-up the dowry custom all together, while some women's rights groups agitated for a legislation declaring dowry giving and accepting as an anti-social and criminal act. Many women's groups sprang up to provide moral and legal support to women who suffered dowry related physical violence or mental cruelty from their husbands or in-laws. The Police in major cities also had to set-up special squads to deal with such incidents. If someone was charged, the women activists also closely monitored the court case to ensure that the culprit did not get off by using bribe or influence.

It must be emphasized that the *bride burning* is limited to the major cities, and is not a common every-day occurrence throughout India. It is a serious criminal act committed only by some greedy families, and is not in any way a religious issue.

THE ABORTION ISSUE

According to Hindu scriptures, the destroying of an embryo is a sinful act. The Hindu code of law, *Manusmriti,* condemns those who perform abortions, and the women who abort their pregnancies. It recommends ex-communication of such people until they perform penance to cleanse themselves of this sin. However, abortions are not uncommon among Hindus, both in India and Canada. Like many other societies, abortions have been used by unmarried mothers to terminate their pregnancies since unwed mothers and illegitimate children are considered outcasts shunned by the society. Today, abortions are also used as a family planning device. In India, abortion is neither illegal nor a political issue.

Hinduism promotes gender equality, as the *Manusmriti* (9.130) declares, "A son is just like one's self, and a daughter is equal to a son. How can someone else take (father's) property when she stands for his self." However, like most societies in the world, having a son is considered very important in traditional Hindu families for various reasons: he carries the family name; after the daughters get married and leave the family, the eldest son takes charge as the head of the joint family unit upon his parents' death; when parents become old or disabled, it is the responsibility of the sons to take care of them. Therefore, a couple will keep on having children until a son is born. In many cases, this practice results in very large families.

Most recently, with the advent of gender identification during pregnancy, some couples in India who only have female offsprings, and are desperate to have a male child while keeping the size of their family small, two or three children, decide to terminate the pregnancies until a male child is conceived. This practice is more common among middle class urbanites in India than among Hindu Canadians. In Canada, most Hindus practice birth control after having two or three children regardless of their gender; it is not uncommon to see Hindu parents with two or three daughters and no sons, and they love their daughters very much.

9.

SCRIPTURES AND SACRED BOOKS OF HINDUISM

All major religions of the world have a holy book which contains the teachings, commandments and philosophies of their founders or prophets. Hinduism is different in this respect. In ancient India, all aspects of knowledge, religious or secular, were considered sacred. Therefore, Hindus are the inheritors of a large body of literature they consider sacred. Since Hinduism is an evolutionary religion, and does not have a specific founder, this knowledge developed over several centuries in ancient India, including pre-historic times. Being a religion that promotes freedom of choice, its adherents are free to accept them all or reject some and accept others. No Hindu is ever persecuted or declared an infidel for rejecting or criticizing the holy scriptures.

SRUTI AND SMRITI:

The ancient Hindus classified their sacred knowledge into two categories:

1. The divine knowledge or eternal truths directly revealed by God Himself, called *'Sruti'* meaning *'that which is heard'*, at the beginning of the creation to some highly advanced seers, Rishis, who were totally sinless and pure, when they were in deep and intense meditation.

2. The other body of religious literature, called 'Smriti' meaning 'that which is remembered'—, created by man and passed on generation to generation as traditions. Smritis include commentaries on or explanation of previously re-

vealed divine knowledge, grammar, law, astrology, phonetics, epics and a great deal more.

VEDAS, THE DIVINE KNOWLEDGE FOR HUMANITY

Literally, the word 'Veda' means 'knowledge'. There are four Vedas that are considered as Srutis, a body of revealed divine knowledge:

1. **Rig Veda** 1028 hymns to God and His various manifestations.
2. **Yajur Veda** Knowledge of rites
3. **Sama Veda** Knowledge of chants
4. **Atharva Veda** Knowledge given by Seer Atharvan

Each of the four Vedas is sub-divided into four sections.

a. **Samhitas:** Basic texts, hymns, formulas and chants

b. **Brahmanas:** Directions for performance of rituals

c. **Aranyakas:** Emphasize the esoteric meaning of the hymns of Samhitas and spiritual experiences attainable from various religious practices

d. **Upnishadas:** Contain philosophy and spiritual experience; spiritual truths and ways to realize them. There are 108 Upnishadas distributed throughout the four Vedas.

Hindu orthodoxy believes that the Vedas were revealed for the entire humanity, and not for a specific race or group of people. However, Western historians believe that Vedas were composed over a period of thousand years starting from 1500 or 1400 B.C.; even this date is not acceptable to all historians since it is based on the 'Aryan Invasion' theory. Some Indian historians push the date to 2500 B.C. Regardless of the date of origin, Vedas are considered the first and the foremost books of world literature, and the basic foundation and fountainhead of all divine knowledge. According to Pundit Vedalankar, "Vedas are the knowledge of God and there is nothing in it that contradicts the universally accepted laws of science; it is not dependent on divine miracles which defy the law of nature in order to declare its validity and supremacy."

Many eminent non-Hindu and Western scholar have studied the Vedas. The views of some of these scholars are outlined below.

"After gradual research, I have come to the conclusion that long before all heavenly books, God had revealed to the Hindus, through the Rishis of yore, of whom Brahma was the chief, His four books of knowledge, the Rig Veda, the Yajur Veda, the Sama Veda and the Atharva Veda."

Dara Shikoh, son of Shahjahan, the great Moghul Emperor of India who built the famous Taj Mahal.

"If there is a God who has created heaven and earth, it will be unjust on his part if He deprived millions of souls born before Moses of His Divine knowledge. Reason and comparative study of religions declare that God gives his Divine knowledge to mankind from his first appearance on earth."

"Science of Religion", Prof. Max Muller'

"Let us agree that this system of Ethics which I have given I have been unable to give more than the slightest survey, while the first ever known to man (Vedas) is also the loftiest which he has ever practised. As for the primitive traditions, it is true that these affirmations and precepts are the most unsought for, the loftiest, the most admirable and plausible that mankind has hitherto known."

"The Great Secret", Materlink, the Noble Peace Prize winner philosopher of Sweden.

"We have pushed our inquiries as far back in time as the records would permit and have found that the religious and speculative thought of the people was far purer, simpler and more rational at the farthest point we reached in the Vedic age than at the nearest and the latest."

"Teachings of the Vedas", Rev. Morris Phillip.

AUTHORSHIP AND LANGUAGE OF VEDAS

Vedas are not writings of certain authors in the usual sense. Although names of various seers are connected with Vedas, none of them claimed the authorship. They believed that they did not create the Vedic knowledge; they were simply chosen as a medium to receive the particular aspects of the divine and eternal truth. Therefore, Vedas are considered impersonal. Since there was no written language in the beginning, the original recipients orally transmitted the Vedic knowledge to a few specially selected seers. These seers were entrusted with the task of not only memorizing them but also maintaining their originality and authenticity. For this purpose, they used to hold regular seminars and conventions on a regular basis. In this manner, the knowledge of Vedas was retained through oral traditions until it was reproduced in a written form around 700 B.C. Again, there is no unanimity about this date among historians and theologians.

Interpretations of Vedas

All four Vedas have been composed in verses, *Mantras*, in Sanskrit. Since an average person cannot understand Vedas in their original form, countless commentaries and interpretive treatise have been written in Sanskrit and other languages. Therefore, an average Hindu, trying to find the correct interpretation of true Vedic knowledge has a very formidable task. Basically, there are two reasons for this difficulty: the antiquated Language of Vedas, and the method of interpretation.

The Vedas were composed in ancient Vedic Sanskrit, while most commentaries were written in classic Sanskrit. The vast difference between Vedic words and words of classic Sanskrit has resulted, in some instances, in misinterpretation of Vedic Mantras. For example, in Vedic Sanskrit, the word GAU has several meanings- cow, cow's milk or skin, earth, sense organ, ray of sun or speech. Most modern scholars, particularly western writers, have applied their knowledge of classic Sanskrit in interpreting Vedas.

One can derive three types of meanings from Vedic mantras:

1. Adhyatmika i.e spiritual or metaphysical.
2. Adhibhautika, i.e. social or material.
3. Adhidaivika, i.e. relating to nature.

However, Yaska, in his work called *Nirukta*, has emphasized the use of roots for deriving the meaning of the words. Using this method, the above noted three words relates to three classes of meanings, and would mean that Vedic mantras are related to science, social order and statecraft. On the other hand, Acharya Sayana's commentary on Veda has used the interpretation of Vedic words which is related to the requirements of *Yajna* (rituals and sacraments). Generally, Western scholars' work on Vedas has adopted Sayana's approach, but only a few have given a scientific interpretations to Vedic mantras. This difference in interpreting Vedas has caused a lot of confusion. Therefore, most Hindus depend more on Gita and other sacred books, to be discussed later, for Vedic knowledge.

Smritis: Other Sacred Literature

Smritis are a vast body of literature- legal, social, historical, religious and philosophical- composed after Vedas. All Smritis are sacred to Hindus, but they are considered 'man made literature' as distinct from Vedas, the divine revelations. Unlike the Vedas, the Smritis were written by various sages. However, they derived their authority from Vedas. Being the 'man made' literature, Smritis were revised from time to time to make them relevant to current social conditions. The major Smritis include: Sutras, Manu Smriti, Gautama Smriti, Parasara Smriti and Bhagavad Gita.

PURANAS: The literature for masses

The Sanskrit word 'Purana' means 'ancient'. The Puranas, a collection of Sanskrit literature in poetic style, are aimed at explaining the Vedic knowledge to masses and persuading them to lead a virtuous life. Some scholars are of the opinion that, initially, they were created for Shudras who were barred by Brahmins from reading or even listening to Vedas. But, later on, Puranas became universally popular with ordinary people of all castes due to their simple and interesting style, and became 'Vedas for masses' or the 'fifth Veda'. Puranas have been edited, revised and amplified so many times over the centuries that no Purana has a single author or a precise date of its composition. However, some Puranas cite the Sage Vyasa's name as the original author of its stories, but some scholar consider it as an effort to make them as 'divine' knowledge.

Puranas can also be considered a sort of 'encyclopedia' of Hinduism. Through colorful stories, they depict the glory of various aspects of God or divine incarnations but also contain historical accounts, codes of social behavior, moral values, geographical data, philosophical doctrines, knowledge of physics, chemistry and medicine and so forth. They are so varied in subject matter that it would be impossible to categorize them. However, ancient scholars have divided Puranas into ten major categories listed in Bhattacharyya's *Ancient Indian History and civilization*.

1. **Sarga:** description of the creation of world.
2. **Partisarga:**description of the dissolution of the world
3. **Vamsa:**dynastic list of divine incarnations and sages.
4. **Manvantara:** ages of various creations of world.
5. **Vamsanucharita:** the royal dynasties.
6. **Vritti:** different means of earning livelihood
7. **Raksa:** facts about incarnations of God.
8. **Mukti:** liberation or salvation.
9. **Hetu:** unmanifested life.
10. **Apasraya:** knowledge of God.

Although Puranas are numerous, there are eighteen major Puranas, called Mahapuranas: 1. Brahma; 2. Vishnu; 3. Padma; 4. Shiva; 5. Bhagavata; 6. Naradiya; 7. Markandeya; 8. Agni; 9. Bhavishya; 10. Vamana; 11. Linga; 12. Varaha; 13. Garuda; 14. Brahmavaivarta; 15. Kurma; 16. Brahmanda; 17. Matsya; 18. Skanda. There are also eighteen minor Puranas.

The Puranas have personified God into numerous divine characters and woven very colorful stories around them. Over the centuries, these stories have been recited in Hindu homes and temples. Hindu children in India grow up listening to Puranic stories told by their grandparents, and watching dances and dramas in street theaters, based on such stories. In modern India, Puranic stories are being retold through the media of children's comic books, feature films and television serials which are also very popular with Canadian Hindus. In this manner, Puranas have kept Hinduism alive. Without Puranas, Hinduism would have remained confined to Vedic scriptures which Hindu masses could neither read nor comprehend.

However, many modern Hindus hold Puranas responsible for projecting a very distorted image of Hinduism. They claim that the flights of Puranic poets' imagination have been misinterpreted as a true history of 'gods' and 'demons'. In Puranic stories even the rivers, mountains, trees and birds talked like humans, and had divine powers. The story tellers, often priests, never explained the morals, messages and concepts hidden behind the metaphors and parables; they were accepted by the ordinary folks as real events that actually happened in the ancient times. Some Hindu scholars are of the opinion that some of the so called 'gods' may have in fact been the deified leaders of Aryan settlers trying to subdue the natives of India who were portrayed as 'demons'. Consequently, Hinduism has been misconceived as a polytheistic religion of countless strange looking gods and goddesses. For this reason, Hindu children born in Canada cannot relate to the Puranic brand of Hinduism which is still being promoted in most Hindu temples of Canada. Many parents are worried that their children may become turned off from their religion unless efforts are made by Hindu institutions to explain the Vedic form of Hinduism in a simple and logical manner through the medium of the English language.

SUTRAS: The Manuals of scriptural instructions

Literally, the term 'Sutra' means 'thread' but it is believed that its secondary meaning is 'that which is connected' because Sutras present Vedas in the form of a 'manual of instructions' using aphorisms. The Sutra text is aimed at economy of expression i.e. using only a word or a sentence to express a comprehensive meaning. This was a predominant style for expressing and transmitting the rules of grammar, law, rituals, moral codes and philosophy etc. The Sutras were often couched in technical language and required commentaries in order to comprehend them.

THE RAMAYANA

Ramayana is the finest ancient work of poetic literature attributed to Sage Valmiki. It was originally composed in Sanskrit, but numerous versions of Ramayana have been written in every Indian language; Tulsi Ramayana in Hindi and Kambanna Ramayana in Tamil are the most popular ones. The translation of Ramayana is also available in English and many other foreign languages.

The great epic Ramayana relates to the story of Lord Rama (Hindus pronounce it as Ram), the divine king of Ayodhya, considered by most Hindus as an incarnation of God. On the day of prince Rama's coronation, his stepmother compels his father to banish Rama to the forest for fourteen years. Rama goes into exile with his wife Sita and younger brother Lakshmana. While they live there as humble forest dwellers, Sita is abducted and held prisoner by Ravana, the demonic and powerful king of Sri Lanka. When all peaceful methods fail, Rama wages a war against Ravana with the help of tribal chiefs of the area. Rama wins the war and returns to Ayodhya when the exile is over. He is crowned and reigns over Ayodhya which he turns into a utopian state called Ram-Rajya.

Ramayana is more than a folklore or a powerful human drama. It describes in a colorful way the lifestyle and customs of ancient Hindus; its beautiful verses combine the ideals of Hindu morality with politics, law, philosophy and history. It teaches people how to conduct their daily lives applying the virtues exemplified by Lord Rama, Sita and Lakshmana.

From a Western perspective, Ramayana can be considered as a combination of Bible, Shakespeare, the 'Odyssey', the 'Iliad' and much more.

For countless centuries, Ramayana has been a spiritual guiding light for Hindus. The very mention of the word 'Ram' strikes the cord of love and devotion in the hearts of Hindus. They believe that the mere hearing or repeating of his name alone would purify one's soul. In many parts of India, people greet each other with the expressions 'Ram Ram Ji', 'Jai Ram Ji Ki' meaning 'Salutations or victory to Lord Rama.' When Mahatma Gandhi died, the last words he uttered were, 'O Ram'. Hindus children grow up watching with awe and devotion the story of Lord Rama played in street theaters. Most recently, Ramayana has been produced in the form of a TV series. When Ramayana is screened, life in India comes to a standstill; with their eyes glued to the TV screen, Hindus in every household sit still in sheer ecstasy, totally immersed in the love of Lord Rama. To them, it is not just entertainment; it is the modern style of worship and meditation. In Canada, Hindus watch Ramayana on video or Indian TV programs with the same devotion.

MAHABHARATA

The epic of Mahabharata, composed by Sage Vyasa, containing over 90,000 stanzas is the longest single poem in the world. Mahabharata depicts how greed, selfishness and hunger for power leads to injustice, oppression and violence; what sacrifices virtuous people have to make in order to uphold justice and truth; it encourages one to fight and make sacrifices to protect one's rights and justice. A great volume of literature produced in India is based on it. The Indian film industry has produced a TV serial which is as popular as Ramayana and also watched by Canadian Hindus.

Unlike Ramayana, Mahabharata does not portray an ideal society; it is a story of a great war resulting from a clannish feud. The story revolves around a famous royal clan that ruled around the region of modern Delhi. The conflict involves two families, the Kauravas and Pandavas, who were cousins. Using trickery and fraud, Kauravas usurp the kingdom of virtuous Pandavas. After Lord Krishna's mediation fails to resolve the conflict, the war ensues. It is believed that all kings and emperors of the entire South Asian sub-continent joined the battle of Mahabharata; some under compulsion sided with the wicked Kauravas while others fought for the righteous Pandavas. Lord Krishna refused to fight for either side. Instead, he chose to become the charioteer of Arjuna, the mighty Pandava warrior and a close relative, friend and disciple of Lord Krishna.

When the two huge armies faced each other in the battlefield, and the battle was about to begin, the mighty Arjuna became nervous and depressed. He refused to fight, but not because of the fear of his enemies; it suddenly dawned on him that the enemies on the other side included his own kith and kin. Thus, he would have to kill his teacher, uncles, cousins and other relatives in order to win back the kingdom. In despair, Arjuna threw away his arms and sought Lord Krishna's advice regarding righteous and unrighteous deeds. In the middle of the battle ground, Lord Krishna had to deliver his sermons in order to motivate Arjuna to fight for his rights by convincing him that the battle he was about to fight was between righteousness of the Pandavas and wickedness of the Kauravas, and it was his duty to uphold the former. The mighty Arjuna and his smaller army won this great battle of Mahabharata, but at a great cost of devastating loss of human lives on both sides. Many Hindus compare the battle of Mahabharata with the two World Wars of the modern age. Some scholars believe that beside the socio-economic catastrophe it caused in India, Mahabharata was the beginning of the disintegration of the Hindu value system. However, it was this battle which gave the Hindus the Bhagavad Gita, the compilation of Lord Krishna's sermons to Arjuna.

THE BHAGAVAD GITA: THE HINDU *"BIBLE"*

Over the centuries, the Bhagavad Gita, meaning 'divine songs', has become so popular that it has been nicknamed as the 'Hindu Bible'. A small book of 700 verses in Sanskrit language, Gita depicts the dialogue between Lord Krishna and the mighty warrior Arjuna. During this dialogue, Lord Krishna summarizes the teachings of Vedas and Upnishadas, and explains the gist of Hindu philosophies. It also serves the purpose of a practical manual for daily living in any age. The verses of the Gita touch every aspect of human life on this earth; it emphasizes people's moral obligations and duties (Dharma) under various sets of circumstances in their lives; it answers the fundamental questions and the meaning of life and death; It explains the law of Karma and reincarnation; it outlines the purpose of human life on this earth and points to various ways to attain the ultimate goal of liberation from the cycle of birth and death. Gita is a practical guide on the science of living. Like Arjuna, when a Hindu faces a complex problem and becomes depressed, instead of running to a psychiatrist, he finds peace, solace and inspiration by reading Gita. For centuries, Gita has offered spiritual strength to Hindus. Mahatma Gandhi summarizes the value of Gita in his own life in the following manner:

"When disappointment stares me in the face and all alone I see not one ray of light, I go back to the Bhagavad Gita. I find a verse here and a verse there and I immediately begin to smile in the midst of overwhelming tragedies- and if they have left no visible scar on me, I owe it all to the teachings of the Bhagavad Gita."

The influence of Gita, translated into English and many other foreign languages, has travelled far beyond the borders of India. Gita has impacted the thoughts of many famous western scholars and philosophers. When the nuclear physicist Robert Oppenheimer was overwhelmed by watching the stunning glow of the atom bomb explosion in the testing grounds of New Mexico, he recalled the following verse of Gita (11.12):

"If the lights of a thousand suns were to blaze all at once in the sky, it would be the splendor of that great Being."

THE UPANISHADAS:

The Sanskrit word 'Upanishad' literally means 'to sit near'. Max Muller interprets it as the act of sitting beside a teacher from whom the pupils acquire secret knowledge through dialogue, discussion and debate. According to Basham, it means 'a session' sitting at the feet of a master who imparts esoteric doctrines. Over the centuries most of the Upanishadas were lost, however, at present there are 108 Upanishads of which 11 are considered most important. The Upanishadas are the last parts of the Vedas in which spiritual masters interpret, illuminate and crystallize the Vedic philosophies in simple forms of communication i.e. dialogue and debate. They are also referred as Vedantic philosophies meaning the sum total of Vedic doctrines.

Upanishadas are monotheistic, and talk about God, matter and soul. They answer all questions the most fertile human mind can ever conceive about God, soul, human life, universe and the world beyond. For example, the awesome simplicity of Upanishads is reflected in the following dialogue in which the meaning of soul is explained in Chandogya Upanishad.

"Fetch me a fruit of the banyan tree."
"Here is one, sir."
"Break it."
"I have broken it, sir."
"What do you see? "
"Very thin seeds, sir."
"Break one."
"I have broken it, sir."
"Now what do you see."
"Nothing, sir."
"My son, what you do not perceive is the essence, and in that essence the mighty banyan tree exists. Believe me, my son, in that essence is the Self of all that is. That is the truth, that is the Self. And you are that Self."

SHAD-DARSHANAS (SIX SYSTEMS OF PHILOSOPHY)

The intellectually inclined Hindus of the ancient times did not blindly accept the sacred doctrines revealed to their sages. For centuries, lively and fiery debates have been the notable feature of intellectual life. The discussions centered around metaphysical issues: Is there a creator; what is the relationship between God, matter and soul; how was this world created; What was the cause of creation; how can we realize God and attain salvation. This intellectual approach to seeking truth culminated into six systems of Hindu philosophy, each considered equally valid, called 'Shad-Darshanas'; 'Shad' means six and 'Darshana' means `observation and a close examination.' The six systems or doctrines outlined below reflect the plurality and diversity in Hindu thoughts.

1. ***Nyaya*** (Analysis) system, credited to the great teacher *Aksapada* Gautama, is based on logic, and promotes the concept that clear thinking, reasoning and logical argument were necessary for attaining salvation.

2. ***Vaisesika*** (Individual characteristics) system, authored by Uluka Kanada, is a kind of atomic philosophy and deals with physics. Its proponents assert that nature is atomic, atoms are distinct from the soul, and each element possesses particular characteristics which differentiate it from the four non-atomic substances- mind, soul, time and space.

3. ***Sankhya*** (Enumeration) school was founded by the legendary sage Kapila, and resembles atheism. Although it acknowledges the existence of soul and matter, it recognizes 25 basic principles called *Tattva*, of which the first one is "matter" called *Prakriti*. The evolution, rather than creation, resulted not from a divine cause, but it is inherent in the nature of Prakriti. This principle was modified during the middle ages in order to purge its atheistic element.-

4. ***Yoga*** (Union or application) school of philosophy credited to Patanjali proposes that a complete control over the senses and body will lead to divine realization. This concept is discussed in detail in another chapter.-

5. *Mimansa* (Inquiry) system was founded by Jaimini with the purpose of explaining the Vedas, reasserting that they contain divine knowledge, and are eternal. The other scholars after him developed their own concept of salvation for which they considered the knowledge of the Vedas as a pre-requisite. Eventually, this school of thoughts merged with the Vedanta system.

6. *Vedanta* (End, Essence or Conclusion of Vedas) philosophy is the most significant and current of all other systems. Its followers claim that the other five were parts of the evolutionary process, and the Vedanta is the final product. The Vedantic philosophy has its roots in the Vedas that are considered sacred and unquestionably true. It proposes that an individual is more than just a total sum of mind, body and ego; a soul that dwells in a person is divine; any person can discover this divinity through spiritual practices. Although the credit for the origin of this philosophy goes to sage Vyasa, it was popularized by Sankara (788-820).

10.

THE CORE BELIEFS OF HINDUISM

The most striking feature of Hinduism is pluralism. It is an amalgam of many beliefs and traditions; it synthesizes diverse viewpoints, while blending and assimilating the ideas of many races and cultures that made India their home. However, it does not mean that Hindus do not have universal beliefs. Underneath the diversity of beliefs and practices there is a common thread of characteristic concepts which bind them together. This chapter deals with the basic tenets acceptable to all Hindus.

THE CONCEPT OF GOD

Hindus believe in one Supreme God, *Brahman* (not to be confused with the *Brahmin* caste), a divine conscious energy, both innate and transcendent, the creator of the entire universe, the sole cause behind everything seen or unseen, moveable or immovable; He creates, sustains and dissolves everything. The word "Brahman' has its root in the verb 'bruha' meaning 'to pervade', and therefore Brahman means that which pervades the whole universe. According to Hindu scriptures, He has many attributes: He is omniscient; He is omnipotent; He is omnipresent; He is self-proven; He is eternal; He is in this world and beyond it; He has no beginning, no end; He is second to none. Hindus call this infinite Supreme Reality *Satchidananda,* which is a combination of three Sanskrit words; *Sat, Chit* and *Anand* which means that God is absolute existence (or being), absolute consciousness and absolute bliss. The Vedas describe Him as 'neti, neti' because 'not by speech, not by mind, not by sight' can He be reached. He is an ecstatic experience of highest bliss, continuous and beyond time and space.

ONE GOD BUT MANY NAMES

Hindus are often puzzled and amazed when non-Hindus ask them, "Who is *your* God ?" Hindus believe that people with different cultures understand the same One Supreme God in their own way and have different names for Him: Christians call Him *our Father in heaven;* Muslims call Him *Allah.* Hindus have countless names for Him as His attributes and characteristics are infinite. Swami Dayanand Saraswati, the great Hindu reformer, gives etymological interpretations of one hundred names for God in his famous work *Satyarth Prakash, Light of Truth*. Some of the most common Hindu names for God are given below with their meanings:

Ishwar:	The almighty Lord of the universe.
Prabhu:	The Lord of all beings.
Paramatma:	The Supreme Soul.
Parameshwar:	The most powerful.
Brahman:	The one who exists in everything.
Brahma:	The Creator of the universe.
Vishnu:	The one who sustains.
Shiva:	The one who does good to all.
Mahadeva:	The one who is most illustrious.
Bhagwan:	The one who is object of adoration and worthy of reverence.

POLYTHEISM, A PROFOUND MYTH

The above Hindu concept of One God may puzzle some readers as they must have often heard or read that Hindus worship a multitude of gods and goddesses. This profound misconception is so pervasive and has been perpetuated for so long in the Western world that it may be extremely difficult for many readers, including some Hindus, to believe otherwise. One incident would indicate that the ignorance of the Hindu idea of *One God but many names* and forms thrives even in very high places. In February 1988, a multi-faith service was held in Toronto to celebrate Heritage Day. About one thousand Canadians of all religions were in attendance. Hindu Canadians were shocked to find that their leaders were not allowed to address the gathering. When asked about this omission, the Coordinator of the event, a Christian clergy, responded that Hindus did not qualify as their religion was not monotheistic.

What is the origin of this myth ? Basically, it stems from the misinterpretation of the Vedas which has been dealt with in another chapter of this book. The early compositions of Rig Veda do sing the glory of various Devas; *Agni* (fire), *Mitra* (friend or ally), *Indra* (king of Devas), *Varuna* (Water), *Yama* (death), *Rudra* (storm), *Chandra* (moon), *Surya* (sun) etc. The Sanskrit word Deva means *Illuminate* or *lustrous* and has at least fifteen other meanings, but it has been incorrectly translated as 'god' in English. The ancient Hindus were pre-occupied with nature, but they considered the aforementioned *Devas* as manifestations or representations of God, not as separate divine entities. They saw the spirit of the same Supreme Being in all those natural phenomena. According to *Mundaka-Upanishada,*

"Brahman has caused the show of the creation of the vast universe, which is very helpful to have some idea of the limitless magnitude, glory and the resplendent nature of the transcendent, uncontaminated, and impersonal Being. Fire is the form of Him; heaven is his head; the sun and the moon are His eyes; the quarters His ears; the Vedas His speech; the wind His breath; the whole world His heart; the earth His feet. He is the infinite God, known as *Vishnu,* the inner soul of all beings. From Him is born the sun, who is merely burning fuel in that great Fire; from Him comes forth the rains which produce herbs and corn, and valour in men and women; from whom are born the various people."

The Hindu scriptures have more than ample evidence to prove that Hinduism is monotheistic. Vedas and other scriptures emphatically refer to a **singular** Supreme Being. We quote some sources to debunk the myth of Hinduism as a polytheistic religion.

"The One Existence the wise call by many names as Agni, Yama, Matarishwan." (Rig Veda 1.164.46)

"Our Father, our Creator, our Disposer, who knows all positions, all things existing; who is only One, bearing names of different qualities. Him other beings seek by questioning." (Atharva Veda ii.1.3)

"He is one indeed (Eka Eva); there is no second, third fourth or tenth; He is only ONE." (Atharva Veda 13.4.16)

"God is all pervading, lustrous, flawless, pure, sinewless, free of sins, all knowing, existing in all, transcendental, ever-living and self-proven." (Yajur Veda 40.8)

"He is called *Brahma*-the Creator of the universe; *Vishnu*-All-pervading or sustainer; *Rudra*-Punisher of the wicked, whom he causes to weep: *Shiva*-blissful and benefactor of all; *Akshara*- Immortal, omnipresent; *Swarat*- Self-effulgent; *Kalagni*- Cause of the dissolution of the world and regulator of the time; *Chandrama*- true source of happiness." (Kaivalya Upanishad)

"Being All-glorious, some call Him *Agni*. Being embodiment of all true knowledge, other call Him *Manu*. Other call Him *Indra*, being All-powerful and Protector of all. Others *Prana*, as the source of all life. Others, again, call Him *Brahma*, Greatest of all beings." (Manu Smriti XII 122, 123)

Thus, the Hindus believe in the principle of *Unity in Diversity*. The sages whose one concern was with man's world recognized that man in his limited understanding might worship various gods but behind this worship lies the worship of One. The idea that the universe is the dwelling place of the Lord or the Lord is the in-dweller of everything is expressed in the great verse of the Isavasyopanishad·

"Whatever moveable or transient thing is there in the world, all that is to thought of as pervaded by Isha or the Lord."

Finally, we quote Saint Ramakrishna Paramhans who sums it up so beautifully:

"Many are names of God and infinite the forms that lead us to know Him. In whatsoever name or form you desire to call Him, in that very form and name you will see Him."

DEVAS (DEITIES): THE MINISTERS AND ANGLES OF GOD

Hindus also worship God through many male and female deities, called *Devatas* and *Devis*, which leads to the misunderstanding that Hinduism is a polytheistic religion. This concept can be best explained by drawing an analogy.

The Queen of England is the sovereign head of Canada, and we are ruled by a government in Her Majesty's name. She is represented by the Governor General of Canada, but the country is governed by the Prime Minister and his numerous ministers. When we write to the government on a specific issue we do not write to the Queen. Generally, we would deal with the minister who is responsible for that specific subject. If we want something done, we have to win the favour of Her Majesty's minister. Similarly, God also runs His Kingdom through various Devatas, His *Angels* or *Ministers*, who draw their power from Him. They are erroneously called gods. These deities are invisible, divine and ageless, but they are all subordinate to God.

In this manner, most Hindus worship God through His ministers, manifestations and representations to which they have assigned different names. Over the centuries, interesting stories have spun around them. Every family or village has its favourite deity called *Isht-Devata* or *a chosen deity*. For an ordinary person, it is much simpler to carry a known image of God in the mind than an abstract one. Hindus believe in one intangible Supreme Being, but worship Him through the image, and do not worship the image as God. Hindu literature talks about 330 million deities. Since each person may conceive God differently, there can be as many images or representations of God as the number of people on this earth. Perhaps, the author of this concept believed that the world population in his or her time was 330 millions; since no one had seen God, each person held a *personalized* image of

Him in his mind; hence, there are 330 million chosen gods. However, this idea gives the wrong impression that Hindus practise polytheism. Many Hindus themselves find it hard to comprehend this concept of *Unity in diversity.*

THE AVATAR (GOD ON EARTH) CONCEPT

A large majority of Hindus subscribes to the concept of *Avatar*, which means ***one who descends or comes down.*** They believe that God can and does come down to this earth in different forms from time to time. The circumstances that compel Him to do so are described in Gita (IV 7-8):

"Whenever Dharma (righteousness) declines and unrighteousness flourishes, I incarnate, O' Bharata."

"I incarnate age after age, for the protection of the good and destruction of the wicked, and for re-establishment of Dharma."

God has to take a form again and again, for people forget His message and go astray. He comes in flesh and blood to remove the veil of ignorance, and set them on the right course. Hindus believe that by taking birth, God's power does not diminish as he is omnipotent. The type of form he takes depends on the time, place and circumstances. Since Hindus believe in the evolutionary theory of creation, each divine incarnation fulfills the demand of the stage of evolution that exists at a particular time. His nine incarnations- *Matsya* (fish), *Kurma* (tortoise), *Vraha* (boar), *Narsimha* (man-lion), Vamana (dwarf), Lord Rama, Lord Krishna and Buddha- symbolically represent the evolution of earth, life and society. It is believed that the tenth divine incarnation is yet to come to complete the evolutionary process, and start a new cycle.

MESSENGERS OF GOD

Not all Hindus subscribe to the *Avatar* concept. Many believe that God is formless, and does not take birth Himself to show us the right path. Instead, he sends his special messengers or emissaries like Rama, Krishna, Buddha,

Moses, Christ and Gandhi. Since these people possessed extra-ordinary powers, beyond the comprehension of human beings, they can be considered as God-like people, but not God in flesh and blood. This viewpoint is particularly strong among Hindus who follow the *Protestant* movement called *Arya Samaj.*

THE CREATION OF THE UNIVERSE

Who created this world? Why was it created? How was it created? These questions have stirred the human mind ever since the first human being became aware of his surroundings. However, the Hindu sages of ancient times were the first one to provide the scientific answers in the Vedas. According to Hindu belief, God is the cause of all creations. To create is God's nature; he expresses and manifests Himself through His creation; creating is God's *Leela* or *Sport.* The process of creation has been explained in Hindu literature through the media of interesting stories, metaphors and parables but they all support the concept that God created the universe through a scientific process. It is noteworthy that Hinduism does not quarrel with science which is considered a process with which God created the universe. Unlike the Jewish and Christian teachings, Hindus do not believe that the universe was created out of nothing. Before the creation, the primordial matter, called *Prakriti*, was present but it was still and inert. With His intense desire to create, called *Tapas*, God activated or stirred the atoms of this matter and turned it into a fiery ball of lustrous matter called the *Hiranya Garbha* or the *Golden embryo.* In an effort to explain this complicated process to ordinary people, the creation of the universe is also described, metaphorically, as a result of the *Cosmic Intercourse*, the desire being the seed. According to Rig Veda:

"In the beginning there was darkness, intensified darkness, indistinguishable darkness, all this visible world was reduced to its primordial nature. This primordial world that was enveloped by the all pervading power of One before whom the world of matter is trifle became One (i.e. came into existence through the force of His intense activities- *Tapas.* (10.129.3)

"In the beginning desire arose. This was the first seed of the mind (of the Creator). Those who can see beyond by putting their mind in the heart (i.e. by putting their mind and heart together) found the binding link of the existent in the non-existent (i.e. the non-existent was present in the existent).
(10.129.4)

"The rays of desire spread across the whole world. They spread below and above and the result was that small and big organisms bearing seeds were born. As the existence of the Earth was dependent on the desire of the Creator, the position of the matter was lower than the spirit which acted with desire." (10.129.5)

As the creation evolved scientifically, and this world became inhabitable, God created the first group of human beings, men and women, without the process of conception in the same way as trees were first created without seeds. Thereafter, He set the Law of Nature in motion to govern His creation.

The quest of the Vedic sages was also concerned with the dissolution of the world. It is believed that the world goes into an on-going cycle of creation and dissolution. At the time of dissolution, all things like sun, moon, earth planets disintegrate and turn into tiny invisible particles that fill the whole space. Each new creation evolves from the 'seeds' of the previous one, grows, flourishes, drop seeds to create the next universe and dies. The present universe was created about 2000 million years ago, and is presently in its dying stage. The modern Hindu seers believe that the current state of affairs- depletion of natural resources, ecological disasters, development of weapons of mass destruction, acute obsession with sensual pleasures and degradation of moral standards- certainly points in that direction.

THE JIVATMA (INDIVIDUAL SOUL OR 'SELF'):

" Who am I? " Thousands of years ago, the ancestors of Hindu Canadians pondered this question that still concerns us today in North America. The result of their search for the answer is found in the concept of *Atman* which means Self or Soul. The Self is defined as a subtle, invisible and conscious life force, an energy or element that dwells in the body is called *Jivatma* or *Atman* which means the individual soul or `self'. The body itself is not the *Jivatma.* Hindus consider the body as the house where Jivatma resides, but Man is not the body with a soul; Man is THE SOUL in a body. Like the Supreme Soul, the individual soul is immortal and has no gender. In the Gita, Lord Krishna describe the attributes of the individual soul or the `Self' in the following manner:

"Weapons cannot cut it; fire does not burn it; waters do not drench it; nor does the wind wither it." (Gita 2.23)

Interestingly, Christ also reaffirmed the concept of soul and its immortality when he said, "Fear not them that kill the body, but are not able to kill the soul."

All living and conscious things have a soul which acts according to the body it resides in. Life starts when a soul enters a body, and death occurs when it leaves the body. The soul has three attributes: 1. Aptitude to know; 2. Aptitude to create; 3. Aptitude to enjoy. However, the ordinary individual soul has limited power to know and create.

Hinduism's answer to the question "who am I?" is, "Aham Brahmasmi." meaning "I am Brahman, the perfect Spirit." or "Tat tvam asi." which means "Thou are THAT". Here, THAT refers to God. In other words, the individual soul in our body is the part and parcel or essence of the Supreme Soul. Since Brahman is the source of Atman, they are one and the same; latter is a tiny fraction of the former. If Atman is the amount of electricity that runs a radio, the God is the total sum of electricity generated by the entire hydro network. One might ask, "If God, the Universal Soul, is the origin of our human soul, why is then the latter weak or imperfect." According to Hindu belief, While living in the body, the soul is imperfect as it performs both good and bad actions; it enjoys the fruits of its good actions and suffers for the bad actions. The imperfections and impurity of the individual soul stem from many sources: cravings for, and attachment to material things, desires for sensual gratification, jealousy, egoism, lust, greed, likes and dislikes. However, Hindu seers believe that by the discipline of Yoga the individual soul can attain the state of perfection.

PUNARJANMA (REINCARNATION)

After death, the body is cremated or buried. But, what happens to the soul after it leaves the body ? The answer lies in the Hindu concept of *Life after Death (Punarjanma)*, also called as *Transmigration of Soul.* According to Hindu belief, it is the body that dies, not the soul. The soul is immortal. After the soul abandons a body, it migrates to a brand new (as yet unborn) body. This is known as *rebirth* or *transmigration of soul.* According to Gita (2.22):

> " Just as a person discards old and tattered clothes and puts on new ones, the soul discards the old or weak body and enters a new one. "

There are two theories of reincarnation. According to one school of thought, the soul, after going through 84,000 animal species, finally acquires a human body by virtue of good Karmas. Further incarnations are then in human forms only. The second school of thoughts subscribe to the theory that we do not necessarily reincarnate as human beings all the time. We may be born as any living thing; a bird, animal or insect. We all carry the burden of our good or bad deeds to the next life. A person who acts like an animal in his human life may return to this world as an animal. This cycle of rebirth ends when the soul merges into its source of origin, Brahman, the Universal Soul or the Absolute Spirit. This state is called Mukti, Moksha or Nirvana which means Liberation from attachment, and at peace with everything

It may be of interest to note that most of the world's religions believe now or once believed in the concept of life after death. The early Christians too believed in reincarnation until King Justinian took it out of the Bible. Many statements in the Bible clearly reflect the concept of reincarnation. In the following lines Christ declared that John the Baptist was the reincarnation of Elias:

"But I say unto you, that Elias has come already, and they knew him not." (Matthew 17-12); "Then the disciples understood that he spoke unto them John the Baptist." (Matthew **17.13**)

Many modern Christians have started going back to their old teachings. The famous actress Shirley MacLaine has made reincarnation popular in North America. In general conversations, people often use phrases like, "I must have known you in a previous life," or "See you in a next life." There have been many documented cases of *out of body* experiences and detailed memories retained from a previous life. Many of these reported incidents have been investigated and validated by skeptical journalists, scientists and psychologists.

THE LAW OF KARMA (ACTION)

Sometimes we see a wicked and dishonest person enjoying the good life without working very hard, and also come across another person who is honest, decent and hard working, yet he is living a very miserable life. When we compare the two, we are often puzzled and ask, " Where is the justice?" Hindus find the answer in the *Law of Karma;* Karma means actions, deeds or work. The Hindu concept of Karma is based on the natural law of *Cause and effect*; every action has an equally strong reaction. Therefore, Karma is the cause of all effects; it explains all the pleasures and pains we experience in life

According to this principle, each person reaps the good or bad fruits in his or her present life in accordance with the good or bad Karmas accumulated during his or her previous lives. Although the results of unethical behavior may not become obvious immediately, one can never escape the consequences of one's action; *as you sow so shall you reap*. This is the divine system of justice, based on the principle of *cause and effect*. The Law of Action explains that the apparent injustice, the obvious inequality in wealth or capabilities results from the varying actions that individuals indulged in their immediate or distant pasts. Our good deeds also dictate the quality of life we will have, and the type of body (human, bird or animal) our soul will have in the next birth. In this way, the Law of Action is inter-twined with the concept of ***Rebirth or Transmigration of Soul***.

Unfortunately, there are many decent and honest people who suffer as a result of bad Karmas accumulated in the previous lives. The law of Karma does not say that they should sit idle and suffer as a punishment for the deeds of the previous life. They are not prevented from improving their present condition. Even if their suffering is not instantly alleviated by doing good deeds in the present life, they can still hope for better times once their good deeds wipe out the past bad deeds. In this manner, the concept of Karma not only rationalizes the present sufferings, it also offers hope for the future. The Law of Karma also inspires Hindus to offer help to other suffering souls as, by doing so, they help themselves by earning good Karmas to improve their own lot in the future. "It is the duty of everyone to dedicate his life, intelligence, wealth, words, and his work to benefit other living beings." (Bhagawata Purana 10.22.35). The Law of Karma provides a practical and logical framework for ethical behavior, and keeps the average individual on the right track.

AHINSA (NON-VIOLENCE)

Hindus believe that every living being, including birds and animals, has a soul. Therefore, we must not kill or cause pain to any living creature. This concept is called *Ahinsa,* also pronounced as *Ahimsa,* meaning non-violence. Some Hindus give a much wider meaning to *Ahinsa* than only refraining from killing of or giving physical pain to any living creature; it also includes not causing any emotional trauma or anguish to anyone. Hinduism encourages its adherents to show compassion to all living things. To prove that Ahinsa is more than just a noble theory or belief, Mahatma Gandhi success-fully applied it to India's struggle for independence from British rule. The late Martin Luther King, the civil rights leader in the USA, also borrowed this concept from Mahatma Gandhi.

VEGETARIANISM: The concept of non-violence encourages Hindus to refrain from eating meat as it causes unnecessary destruction of animal life. It must be emphasized that there is no Hindu "Commandment" against eating meat; it is a matter of wisdom. The vegetarian Hindus believe that when God has given them so many other sources of food, it does not make sense to be a meat eater, and become a cause for the killing of innocent animals. Indeed, death of millions of living creatures is inevitable, unavoidable and unintentional as we go about our daily business. It is necessary to kill insects, rodents, and germs that threaten our health and life, but the purpose of *Ahinsa* is to minimize killing, not to stop it completely. By being a vegetarian and refusing to wear fur or leather, one can prevent the slaughter of harmless, innocent creatures. Moreover, even modern nutritionists tell us that vegetarianism is a much healthier lifestyle than meat eating.

It is estimated that about 20 or 30 percent of all Hindus are vegetarians. Generally speaking, the Hindus from southern and western regions of India are more likely to be vegetarians than those from the north.

SACRED COW: Most Hindus who eat meat do refrain from consuming beef as they hold special reverence for cow, but they do not worship cow. Many scholars claim that Hindus' reverence for cow has its origin in India's rural economy rather than religion. In the old times, cow was considered crucial to the village economy. To vegetarian villagers, the cow was more than only the source of milk and its by-products; she also produced bullocks to plough the fields and pull the carts; dried cow dung was used as a domestic fuel and as cement to make mud huts. In rural India, a family's wealth was measured by the number of cows it possessed. It did not make any sense to destroy such a valuable economic resource and asset for food, especially when other sources of food were easily available. For this reason, cow protection was actively promoted, and beef eating was condemned. When religious leaders sanctified the idea of protecting the cow, she became a 'sacred' animal. Since the cow was considered a personal asset rather than commercial livestock, she became a domestic animal, and was treated as a part of the family; it was perfectly natural to develop an emotional attachment with her. Over the centuries, Hindus' love and reverence towards the cow became so strong that when a family cow became ill or useless, she was sent to a 'retirement home' called *Gaushala* which was operated by charitable organizations. Even today, killing a useless cow for meat is considered a cruel, callous and inhumane practice. If people can be emotionally attached to their pets like cats and dogs, showing human compassion towards a very useful and domestic animal that has served society so well is not a strange idea.

11.

HINDU CONCEPTS ABOUT HUMAN LIFE

THE PURPOSE OF LIFE

After birth, we grow-up, become educated, find a job, get married, produce children, grow old and die. One may ask, "is this what life is all about ?" When unable to find the answer, many people end up on a psychiatrist's couch. Thousands of years ago, Hindus sages in India pondered the same question. They found that eating, sleeping, sexual activities, pleasures and pains are common in both animals and human beings. The only thing that separates us from animals is our capability to acquire knowledge, both physical and spiritual. The result of their search is found in the Hindu concept of *Moksha or Mukti*, meaning liberation from the repetitious cycle of birth and death, and unification with God. The purpose of life is to attain Moksha by acquiring divine knowledge.

MOKSHA (SALVATION)

Moksha offers immortality, eternal peace and supreme bliss. It is not nothingness or an eternal life of pleasures in heaven. Moksha is the highest goal and ideal of Hindu life. It is a state of perfection and utmost fulfillment. It cannot be termed as dissolution or destruction of the individual self. According to Upanishad, Moksha is:

> "Just like the merging of the rivers into the sea, where they lose their name and form. Similarly, the wise, freed from name and form attains the supreme reality."

Hindus believe that the aim of all religions is to lift us from our worldly mundane existence to the eternal, blissful and immortal essence. It is the *Moksha* of Hindus, the *Nirvana* of Buddhists and *Kingdom of Heaven* of Christians.

Moksha here and now: Although the soul comes to this earth in different forms, human life is the best creation of God and offers the best opportunity for spiritual growth, evolution and attainment of Moksha. Moksha is not an ideal to be experienced only in the next life after we die. It can be experienced and obtained here and now. A person who has achieved Moksha in his lifetime is called *Jivanmukta* or a liberated soul. Such a spiritually enlightened person is sinless, free from all desires, treats friends and enemies alike, full of love for everyone, remains undisturbed by external forces, identifies his soul with the Universal Soul, sees the divine soul dwelling in every living being, stays above religious differences and dogmas, dedicates all his activities to God and performs them without expectations of rewards. In order to achieve Moksha, an average person has to achieve three lesser goals: *Dharma, Artha and Kama*.

DHARMA (MORAL OBLIGATIONS)

In a previous chapter, we have already defined Dharma in its broadest sense. To an average Hindu, it simply means 'moral obligation' or 'virtuous living'. Each person in this world has a network of relationships; spouse, neighbor, friend, parent, brother, sister, employer, employee, and citizen of the country one belongs to, etc. One has the duty to himself and others to do what is expected of him morally and ethically. To discharge such duties is our Dharma. Dharma is more than praying to God: it is our Dharma to be a competent employee, a loyal friend, loving and caring parent, helpful neighbor, loyal and ideal citizen, faithful and loving spouse etc. Dharma raises man above animal nature. Life is uplifted by Dharma which must be reflected in every aspect of our daily living. Prayers, worship, prescribed ceremonies and rituals are simply aids to help us achieve the goal of Dharma.

ARTHA (ECONOMIC ACTIVITIES)

Contrary to common belief, Hinduism is not against material prosperity or wealth, as long as it is acquired through Dharma, and without over-indulgence. It is a human goal to generate and participate in economic activities or public welfare which includes working in some worthwhile job, profession or business. In this way, not only do we satisfy our personal needs, but also contribute to the welfare of society as a whole.

KAMA (WORLDLY DESIRES)

Kama can be defined as satisfaction of worldly desires, including sex. By using his senses, man enjoys the physical pleasures and beauties of this world. His mind is the instrument of sense enjoyment. Man accumulates wealth so that he can satisfy desires. Desire for sex is also Kama, which has not been forbidden in the Hindu way of life. In fact, it is the desire for sex which keeps the divine wheel of creation in motion. Therefore, it is our Dharma to procreate.

In the process of achieving the goal of fulfillment of normal human desires, man can go astray, and may cause social problems. The deadly disease of AIDS, and an alarmingly high rate of divorce in Canada are two examples of over-indulgence causing social evils. Consequently, Hindu sages have strongly urged the need for a disciplined life. This is why sexual experience is restricted to family life, and pre-marital or extra-marital sex is outside the Hindu norms of human behavior.

Many Hindu scholars believe that Moksha is the only goal of life, and the other three, Dharma, Artha and Kama, are necessary processes an ordinary person has to go through. An ordinary person may have to come to this earth as a human being more than once to achieve Moksha. Regardless of whether or not one attains Moksha, leading a well disciplined life or following Dharma in the process of accumulating wealth (Artha) and fulfilling human desires (Kama) will certainly guarantee a happy life, free of sufferings.

THE FOUR PATHS TO LIBERATION

To enable the spiritual aspirant to attain the state of perfect bliss, Hindu seers evolved the discipline of Yoga. Since each individual is different in mental make-up, aptitude, approach, inclination and temperament, the Hindu system of Yoga offers four paths to choose from:

1. **Dhyana Yoga** -Path of Meditation.
2. **Karma Yoga** -Path of Action.
3. **Jnana Yoga** -Path of Knowledge.
4. **Bhakti Yoga** -Path of Devotion.

DHYANA YOGA- THE PATH OF MEDITATION

Man's mind is restless by nature, always thinking about something or the other. It is filled with desires and wishes, and pre-occupied with enjoying the pleasures of the senses. In this pursuit, man develops many undesirable qualities: anger, jealousy, hatred, greed, over-possessiveness, pride etc. When such thoughts are flushed away, the restless mind becomes calm and tranquil like the unflickering flame of a candle in a windless room. Meditation, through complete control over body and mind, produces one-pointedness and concentrated attention. In a Yoga-state, the purified soul is in communion with God. To reach that advanced and final stage of Yoga called *Samadhi* (blissful equilibrium), takes many years of practice under the close guidance of a Guru, spiritual master. Hindus believe that the ancient sages were in this stage when Vedas were revealed to them.

Many ancient Yogis practised Yoga to acquire superhuman knowledge rather than for salvation. Whatever cynics or skeptics may think of the spiritual claims, numerous experiments conducted by modern medical researchers in recent years have shown some incredible results. An advanced Yogi can: control the rhythm of his own heart-beats, hold his breath for an amazingly long period of time without causing harm to himself, endure extreme heat or cold far beyond the physical capacity of an ordinary person, remain astonishingly healthy on a starvation diet, and be able to perform remarkable physical contortions, and live to more than one hundred years of age with all faculties fully intact. Although ordinary people may not want to invest a significant portion of their lives in order to reach such a high level of accomplishment in Yoga, they can, and do, benefit from Yogic physical exercises, deep breathing and meditation.

Yoga in North America: Yoga is the most recent gift of Hindus to the Western world. Many skeptic medical researchers have confirmed the physical and psychological benefits of yogic exercises and meditation. There are millions of Christians in the USA and Canada who practise some form of Yoga. Educational institutions offer courses in Yoga. Medical doctors routinely prescribe Yoga exercises for muscloskeletal disorders and high blood pressure; psychologists teach meditation to patients who suffer from Chronic pain, migraine headaches, anxiety, 'Burn out' and many other mental disorders. Realising that some non-Hindu patients may object to Yoga's religious connotation, some physicians, psychotherapists and instructors may camouflage Yoga under some other names or expressions.

The credit of popularizing Yoga to North America goes to a Hindu holyman from India, Maharishi Mahesh Yogi, who is nicknamed by the media as the 'Giggling Swami' on account of his peculiar style of talking. He promoted a particular type of meditation, called *Transcendental Meditation* or TM, which is practised by repeating a secret word called *Mantra* given to the student by the instructor. Some orthodox Christian clergies, disturbed by the acceptance and popularity of Yoga among their followers, have started condemning it; one Christian church in the USA called Yoga a *Satanic practice of pagans.* Fortunately, such bleak voices from the wilderness have not deterred Canadians and Americans from reaping the benefits of the non-spiritial aspects of Yoga.

KARMA YOGA- THE PATH OF ACTION

As mentioned earlier, Karma means action, deed or work. There are two types of actions: 1. ***Sakam Karma*** - Actions with selfish motives. 2. ***Nishkam Karma*** - selfless actions.

Sakam Karma: An ordinary person performs actions for results in order to achieve personal goals or satisfy personal desires. Such actions are prompted by selfish motives. A shopkeeper does business to earn profit. A student works hard to get good grades. Such motives are necessary in every day life. According to Hindu philosophy, there is nothing wrong with performing activities for personal rewards or satifaction (called Sakam Karmas) but they are only second best.

Nishkam Karma: An action performed as a sense of moral duty, and without claiming the ownership of its fruit or outcome is called Nishkam Karma. The path of action, Karma Yoga, is concerned with this type of action. When a person does something with a sense of duty and humility, but without a motive, desire or greed for personal gains, he is called Karma Yogi, a performer of selfless actions. Selfless action is performed with love and a sincere desire to serve others.

A Karma Yogi does all his actions without worrying about success or failure. He does not become obsessed with success or failure for two reasons: it may adversely affect his abilities and efforts; every action creates a reaction anyway. Since he has no interest in the results, success does not excite him, and failure cause him no disappointment. By following the path of action, even the day-to-day activities can be elevated to a higher plane when they are performed joyfully as sacred duties dedicated to God. Any kind of work performed in this manner ceases to be burdensome, and becomes a spiritual exercise, a sacred loving sacrifice. This is Karma Yoga, Lord Krishna called it the Yoga of Renunciation, the ladder to Moksha:

> "Whatever you do, whatever you eat, whatever you offer, whatever you give away, whatever austerities you perform....do that as an offering to me. Thereby you will be liberated from the bonds of action, which bear good and

bad results. With your mind firmly set in the Yoga of renunciation, you will become free and come to me."
(Gita: 9.27-28)

Besides being a pathway to Moksha, the concept of Karma Yoga fosters strong work ethics and motivates Hindus to work hard in their daily lives because it is their duty to do so.

JNANA YOGA- THE PATH OF KNOWLEDGE

Man is the most intelligent being created by God. He has the ability to differentiate between good and bad, true and false, real and unreal. He has acquired this ability through knowledge which is a prerequisite for any work. It is through knowledge that we understand this world. Therefore, knowledge has been called light in Vedas: *"Rise from darkness through knowledge."* (Atharva Veda 8-1-8). *Without knowledge, man is like a beast.* Gita says (4.38), *" There is nothing superior to knowledge ."*

There are two types of knowledge, worldly knowledge (like Mathematics, Physics, Chemistry, Economics etc.) and spiritual knowledge. According to Yajur Veda (40.11), both kinds of knowledge are essential: *"by means of science, man attains freedom from disease, by means of spiritual knowledge he acquires salvation."* The secular knowledge we acquire through day to day experiences and by attending schools and universities does not lead to Moksha, it only helps us know the world around us and makes our material life comfortable. The liberation from the cycle of births and deaths lies in divine knowledge. To prepare for this pathway, one has to first learn to control the restless mind through meditation and purify the soul by conquering the five enemies: 1. craving for material desires and sensual gratification; 2. Anger; 3. greed; 4. attachment to worldly possessions; 5. arrogance and pride. Lord Krishna advises:

"Learn knowledge through humble reverence, through inquiry and through service. The wise seers who have perceived the Truth will teach you that knowledge." Gita (4.34)

An intelligent person, possessed with contemplative bent of mind, may choose to seek Moksha through the path of Knowledge. Such a person would analyze and rationalize the nature of everything around, including the Self. After years of contemplation, studying of holy scriptures under the guidance of a spiritual mentor, and practising the knowledge thus gained, a person reaches a stage where he identifies his own soul with the soul in every other being and the Universal Soul. Since he realizes that the same soul dwells in every being, he sees divinity in everything around him, and all differences dissolve. He conquers all human limitations, holds no malice for anyone and is above and beyond religious differences. Such a man of super-consciousness attains Moksha in his own life. He is called *Jivanmukta* (a liberated soul, free from all desires). Jnana Yoga is knowledge, practice and realization all rolled into one. This is the most difficult and the longest path to follow, but according to lord Krishna the rewards are high:

"Those whose ignorance is destroyed by the knowledge of the Self, that knowledge illuminates the Supreme Self like the sun. With thoughts absorbed in That (the Supreme), with the Self fixed on That, making That their whole aim, going toward That, they go to the path that has no return, for their sins have been washed away by knowledge."

(Gita 5.16-17)

BHAKTI YOGA-THE PATH OF DEVOTION

Bhakti is derived from the Sanskrit word *Bhaj* which means 'to be attached to'. To people who neither have patience to study scriptures to discover divine truth nor have intellectual capacity or inclination to do so, Hinduism recommends Bhakti Yoga, the path of devotion. To worship God or offer Him prayers with intense faith, love and devotion is called *Bhakti*. In Bhakti, the fervent devotion to one's personal deity replaces the cool contemplation on formless or the abstract Supreme Being. The path of devotion is simple, it can easily be followed by an uneducated labourer or a university professor. The essence of Bhakti is in sincere prayer which establishes direct communication with God through the medium of *Ishta Devata*, the personal deity. The pre-requisite for following the Bhakti path is faith, Shraddha, as Lord Krishna himself said:

"In whatever form a devotee seeks to worship Me with faith, in that form I sustain his unwaivering faith."

(Gita 7.21)

"However, the ignorant one who has no faith, and is full of doubt, perishes. For he who doubts, there is neither this world, nor the world beyond, nor happiness."

(Gita 4.40)

Bhakta, or devotee, is a man who totally surrenders himself to the will of God and becomes intoxicated with love for Him. When he sits in front of the idol or picture of his *personal* God, *Ishta Devata,* he feels like an innocent child sitting in his mother's lap experiencing sheer bliss. He sees all human virtues in God, and yet considers Him free from all human limitations. He finds peace and ecstasy of love in singing His praises and repeating His name. A Bhakta dedicates all his actions to God,. becomes fearless, and abandons egoism and craving for worldly pleasures.

Criticism of Bhakti: Since Bhakti is the easiest of all the four paths to attain salvation, and can be followed by a common man, it suits a large majority of Hindus. However, many reformist Hindus condemn the concept of worshipping a personal God through rituals, symbols and idols, as a non-Hindu practice not prescribed by scriptures. Some consider Bhakti as a legitimate means to express one's love for God, but only suitable for uneducated people. Indeed, Hindu scriptures clearly state that an idol is not a substitute for God, and it is only a focal point to still the restless mind. It is accepted by most Hindus that mental worship is superior to image worship but every form of worship begins with an image; an ordinary person cannot conceive God without forming some sort of image in his mind. Many Hindus would argue that people of all religions worship God in some form, but Hindus have the courage to admit it. An idol in a Hindu temple is like a cross in a Christian church. Regardless of the criticism of image worship in the Bhakti system, it opens doors to a spiritual life for ordinary Hindus who are either not intellectually equipped to comprehend the other three paths or may not be motivated to follow them. Achieving salvation through chanting God's name in ecstasy, worshipping an idol or singing the glory of God with sheer devotion may not appeal to a spiritually evolved person, but many Hindus would consider Bhakti as a primary or simple step leading to the other three paths to Moksha. It must also be emphasized that all four paths overlap each other. Initially, a Hindu may choose to follow one of them, but may eventually become interested a little bit of the other three paths as well. Many Hindus claim that their religion has been kept alive over the ages by numerous waives of Bhakti movements; to millions of ordinary Hindus, the exponents of the Bhakti system offered a simple way to love God and keep their faith alive at a time when Hinduism was under tremendous pressure from other religions.

THE FOUR *ASHRAMS* (STAGES) OF LIFE

The ancient Hindus realized that there were certain stages in life when some goals were more important and easily attainable than others- without prioritizing such goals, a person's life would become chaotic. They created a plan by dividing the individual life-span into four stages called *Ashramas* which means 'resting-place'. The sequence of the four stages is: 1. *Brahamcharya Ashram* (Celibacy or Student Stage); 2. *Grihastha Ashram* (Householder Stage); 3. *Vanaprastha Ashram* (Retirement Stage); 4. *Sunnyasa Ashram* (Wandering Pilgrim Stage). According to the Vedas, a person can be expected to live for one hundred years. Therefore, each of the four stages of life covers approximately twenty-five years. Without going through these four stages, one cannot attain salvation.

BRAHMACHARYA ASHRAM- THE STUDENT STAGE:

In order to prepare oneself for life, the acquiring of knowledge is essential. After early childhood, it is the

Shiva

Ganesh

responsibility of parents and teacher to ensure that a child receives a good education, both secular and religious, necessary for material prosperity and spiritual development. During this stage, a student is expected to observe complete celibacy, and live a very disciplined life of self-control and restraint. A student is not to indulge in romance and dating or in marriage; acquiring knowledge is a serious affair and must be pursued in a single-minded fashion.

In the ancient times, students would live in the teacher's household set up in the forest, far away from the residential areas, in simple and natural surroundings. These learning centres, called *Gurukula* or teacher's house, were a sort of foster-home or boarding school run by retired couples who transferred their knowledge, skills and wisdom to youths. While living a spartan life, students grew their own food; they learned trades, languages, science, math etc; they studied holy scriptures, practised Yoga, as well as physical and moral disciplines. The *Gurukulas*, separate for boys and girls, did not charge any fee but were supported by the surrounding villages. The students would return home only after completing their education.

This traditional system of Hindu education has disappeared except for a handful of modified versions of *Gurukulas* which still exist in certain parts of India. Modern India uses the British style of schools, colleges and universities. There are separate schools for boys and girls; some colleges practise gender segregation while others have co-education. In Canada, Hindu parents find it extremely difficult to impose the *Gurukul* type of discipline on their children, but do forbid premarital sexual activities. Canadian Hindus consider their children very studious and well disciplined.

GRIHASTHA ASHRAM- THE HOUSEHOLDER STAGE:

Only after finishing education and finding a job, the young Hindu is expected to married and enter the *Grihastha Ashrama*; getting married is considered a sacred duty of a Hindu. As a housholder, he procreates to perpetuate God's creation and produces wealth for both the family and society. The housholder enjoys the worldly pleasures and the fruits of his hard labour but he is cautioned against over-indulgence. Giving financial support to social and religious institutions is a moral obligation of every Hindu household. This stage is given great importance in Hinduism as it is the householder who financially sustains the three other stages and society through taxation and donations.

Hindus consider family as the basic unit of society. Hindus are family oriented people and provide a very secure, caring and peaceful family environment for their children. They are expected to take care not only of their immediate family members but also the retired parents, grandparents and unmarried brothers and sisters.

VANAPRASTHA ASHRAM- RETIREMENT STAGE:

When a householder has discharged his obligations towards his family and society, he then turns his focus on the spiritual aspect of his own life. When he feels that his married children are capable of taking over the administration of the household, it is time to retire. In a joint family system, the senior householder and his wife start loosening their family ties, and let the eldest son and the daughter-in-law make all the decisions; they become consultants and advisers to them. The arrival of a grandchild is generally the signal for them to withdraw from the domestic and business or occupational activities. This is not the stage to take a cruise, travel around the world or buy a Condo in Florida. Traditionally, the Hindu retirees feel they have outgrown the activities of amusement and entertainment, and must seek higher things in life; they want to reflect, study and meditate.

In ancient India, the couple would set up a humble cottage in the forest, and devote their entire time to spiritual activities like studying the holy scriptures, praying, worshipping, practising religious austerity, meditating intensely, trying to find the answers to questions about God, soul and the nature of the universe, etc. Many such retirees would set up a *Gurukulas* in their cottage to pass on their knowledge and experience to the youths. Today, it may not be practical to retire to the forest. Instead, a simple and austere home away from the family serves the purpose.

Since most Hindus Canadians arrived in Canada as immigrants during the late nineteen sixties and seventies, only a few of them have reached the retirement stage. It is generally observed that those who have retired start making frequent trips to India as pilgrims visiting hundreds of temples and religious places that are scattered across India. They also play more active role in the affairs of their local temple or volunteer their time to Indian or mainstream community organizations. Of course, there are others who do not experience the lure for the spiritual adventure. Instead, they feel now they have the money and time to do the things they could not do while raising a family- just relax, look after the grandchildren, start a new hobby, travel and enjoy the wealth they accumulated during their working lives.

SUNNYASA ASHRAM- THE WANDERING PILGRIM STAGE:

The last stage is *Sannyasa* which means complete renunciation of all worldly things. When a retiree is saturated with spiritual knowledge, and sees oneness of all souls with the Supreme Soul, he turns into a *Sannyasi*, one who has renounced; Gita calls him someone who neither loves nor hates, feels neither pleasures nor sorrows. He gives up everything: his personal identity, including his name and address; all bonds of relationships, relatives, friends etc, money and property, fame and pride. His mind is totally detached from all sources of sufferings and pleasures. He has no fear of death. No one is his enemey, no one a favourite; the entire world is his family.

Wearing an unstitched saffron coloured ankle length robe, and carrying nothing except a begging bowl and a staff, a Sannyasi wanders from place to place with no ultimate destination. During the endless journey, he meditates, prays, and does Yoga for physical and mental fitness. He is also a travelling spiritual teacher. As a service to mankind, he shares his spiritual wisdom and experience with those who would care to listen. He never stays at one place for more than three days. To sustain himself, he accepts alms offered by housholders. In Hinduism, offering alms to a Sannyasi is not in the category of charity given to a beggar; offering food to a wandering holyman is considered a blessing, a privilege and an honour to a householder, as well as a religious duty.

Many people in the West condemn this Hindu concept of asceticism as nothing short of sheer madness, forgetting that Jesus too demanded this type of total renunciation of his own immediate followers. He invited them to give up everything, including family obligations, and follow him. Hindus believe that it is very difficult to discover the real 'self' and attain self-relization while still wrapped in the bonds of worldly relationships and attachments. However, this is a very hard act to follow and only a few Hindus would dare to become a true Sannyasi after the retirement stage.

12.

THE ART OF GOD SYMBOLISM IN HINDUISM

In order to explain something difficult or to make learning interesting, we use various audio-visual aids and techniques. For example, a teacher uses a globe to teach world geography to his students. He points out on the surface of the globe various countries, rivers and mountains, etc. The students know that the globe itself is not the world; it only helps them to understand and appreciate the world in an interesting way. Similarly, in order to make common people understand and realize the glory of formless and infinite God, the Hindus used the art of symbolism. No other people in the world have utilized the art of symbolism so extensively for so many purposes: to express their love for God, to graphically illustrate His powers, to deliver His message for mankind, and to explain His limitless attributes and functions. Over the centuries, poets, painters and sculptors have used their rich sense of imagination to describe the undescribable, and give form to the Formless. The colourful and interesting stories we hear about these deities, and various idols and pictures we see in Hindu temples, are a clever use of the art of symbolism as a simple technique or aid to explain to the ordinary people the glory of God. The Hindu sages recognized the fact that most working people neither had time nor the intellectual ability to reach the depths of thought expressed about the formless Creator in the Vedas. Moreover, symbols make the attributes of deities easily and logically understandable.

However, there are many Hindus who do not make use of the art of symbolism for the purpose of understanding and experiencing God. Instead, they read, understand and follow their holy scriptures or meditate on an *impersonal* or abstract God without focusing on any idol or symbol. Many reformist movements in Hinduism have vehemently denounced the worship of idols and their symbols. They would claim that symbol worship and the rituals associated with it had distorted the true concept of God in Hinduism. Moreover, they assert, it is not validated or sanctioned by the Vedas. Notwithstanding the merits of this argument, it cannot be denied that the large majority of Hindus do worship God through the medium of countless images and symbols. Hence, any discussion on Hinduism would remain incomplete without talking about numerous colourful deities and their symbols.

THE MAJOR HINDU DEITIES

There have been no standard forms worshipped by all Hindus throughout the world. For thousands of years, Hindu artists created many forms of God based on stories of Puranas and other literature. It must be emphasized that different regions in India have their own indigenous deities. In some cases, the same deities may have different names and physical appearances in various parts of India. However, we will discuss the major deities who have been the all time favorite and adorn Hindu temples in most parts of India and Canada. Many of these deities have strange anatomical structures but each feature denotes a concept or a message. All of them hold some objects or weapons in their hands, and stand or ride on something symbolizing some aspects of spirituality. It is emphasized that neither the symbols nor their meanings are fixed or standard. It depends on the artist who created the image, and it is hard to know what he had in mind when he conceptualized it. Each deity also has a consort. Once we accept God's representation in a human form, the concept of allowing a consort to each human representation is not a completely far fetched idea. Moreover, the Vedic traditions accord the highest status and recognition to women, and nothing is considered complete or fruitful without the presence of a woman. Hence, to complete the concept of God in human form, each deity must have a *consort:* Brahma is *married* to Saraswati, Vishnu's *wife* is Lakshmi, and Shiva's *consort* is Parvati.

BRAHMA:

Brahma represents the creative aspect of God. He is shown with four heads, four hands and stands on a lotus. In his four hands he is holding a water-pot (Kamandal), the Veda, a rosary (Mala) and a sacrificial tool (Sruva). These objects are metaphors and denote the following messages or meanings.

Four faces: represents Four Vedas.

Four arms: Four aspects of man's inner personality i.e. mind, intellect, ego and conditioned consciousness.

Veda: Scriptural truths are eternal.

Water Pot: Contains water from the holy river Ganga representing purity of thought and character.

Sacrificial tool: selfless service for the benefit of all living beings.

Rosary: It is round and has numerous beads. The circular shape denotes the fact that God creates the world each time it is dissolved which is an endless process. Each bead represents His new creation.

Standing on a lotus: The lotus grows in muddy and murky water but its surface remains so clean and smooth that not a drop of dirty water stays on it. Therefore, the lotus represents truthfulness and perfect behavior amidst the mud of evils.

This symbolism or the image of God, the Creator, represents a message to His best creation, human beings: control all four aspects of our personality, follow the teachings of four Vedas which are eternal, be pure in thought and character, make sacrifices and give selfless service to all, be cool and pure like the water of river the Ganga, attain tranquility of mind through the practice of Yoga, the world is like murky water that is full of sins but must not influence you, be like a lotus, be truthful and try to achieve perfection.

SARASWATI:

After children are born, they start to learn everything from their mother. She helps them relate to this world; she teaches them how to sit, walk, talk, and behave properly. Therefore, woman as a mother is the first teacher of man. Hindu artists applied this earthly concept to the creative aspect of God as well. Brahma's creation needs spiritual knowledge in order to maintain itself properly; without this knowledge, human beings will be no different than animals. Therefore, Brahma's 'consort' Saraswati comes to his assistance. Mother Saraswati, the embodiment of knowledge, represents the ideal Guru. Literally, the word 'Saraswati' means 'the one who imparts the essence of our own 'Self'.

Hindu worship Saraswati as the goddess of knowledge and learning. She is particularly popular with students and artists. She is depicted as sitting on a lotus and has four hands: in one hand she is holding the scriptures, in the other a rosary; with the other two she is playing Veena, a musical instrument. The significance of this imagery can be explained as follows:

Four arms: Four aspects of man's inner personality i.e. mind, intellect, ego and conditioned consciousness.

Scriptures: Scriptural knowledge alone can enlighten us.

Veena: To help the student be in perfect harmony with the world around him, the spiritual master should first teach him to tune up his intellect and mind.

Rosary: As previously explained

Sitting on a lotus: As previously explained

VISHNU:

God as Vishnu, also called Narayana, sustains this world. Lord Rama and Lord Krishna are considered the incarnation of Lord Vishnu, for they came down to put things in order. Vishnu is depicted in numerous poses, but we will only explain his most popular image. Vishnu's blue coloured body is shown with bright yellow robes. He wears a crown and stands on a lotus. He has four hands each holding an object; a conch (Sankha), spinning discus (Chakra), mace (Gada) and a lotus (Padma). The message behind this imagery can be explained in the following manner:

Blue coloured body: God is infinite like the cloudless blue sky

Yellow dress: Yellow colour symbolizes spring freshness and colorfulness, and also gold. The yellow clothes represent the Lord's love for His creation. He is ever fresh like spring. His creation is precious to Him like gold.

Crown: God is the Lord of the entire universe.

Four hands: stands for mind, intellect, ego and conditioned-consciousness. When God takes human form he comes into contact with this world with all four faculties.

Standing on lotus: As previously explained

Lotus in hand: God urges mankind to uphold purity truthfulness and perfection.

Conch in hand: Represents the primal sound of the begin ning of creation, commonly known as 'pranav'

Discus in hand: Spinning discus is a weapon and represents the time cycle

Mace in downward position: It symbolizes the act of 'knocking down' which means that we are knocked down by disappointments and dissatisfaction when we do not listen to God's call to live a spiritual and virtuous life.

LAKSHMI

Lakshmi, the goddess of wealth, is the 'consort' of Lord Vishnu. Since Vishnu represents the sustaining function of God in the form of a male, He must have a *wife* to share His responsibilities. Since wealth is necessary in order to sustain life on this earth, what can be a better metaphor than associating him with Lakshmi.

The image of Lakshmi usually has four arms, and she stands on a large lotus. She is holding a lotus in each of the two upper hands, and is showering money from the two lower hands. The significance of each symbol is as follows:

The two lotus in hands: Each lotus is held in an upright position. Here one lotus is a metaphor for purity. It means that man must uphold purity both in thought and action. Lotus is also a symbol of detachment as it remains in murky water but its surface is neither wet nor dirty. Therefore, the second lotus stands for detachment.

Showering of money: Lakshmi is showering two types of wealth- material wealth and spiritual wisdom.

Standing on a lotus: As explained previously.

Hence, the message here is that those who uphold purity of thought and action, and are untouched by the mud of evils, are blessed by goddess Lakshmi with material prosperity and spiritual wisdom

SHIVA

God creates this world, sustains it and then dissolves it in order to create a new one. Shiva, also called Mahadeva or Mahesh, represents His function of dissolving this world. Since the dissolution is followed by His new creation, many Hindus consider Shiva as the regenerator and not the destroyer. His images are created in numerous poses including that of ***Dancing Shiva or Nataraja.*** Here we will only describe the significance of his sitting pose and the messages it carries.

Shiva is shown in human form with two hands holding a trident (Trishul) in one and a small drum (Damru) in the other. He wears a serpent around his neck, a garland of skulls as ornaments and three horizontal lines of holy ash (Bhasma) on his forehead which has a third eye in the middle. He sits on a tiger skin with one arm resting on an altar. We also see mother

Ganga entering His hair locks. Each of these symbols carries a specific and meaningful message for His devotees.

Small drum: Represents sound which is the source of language, music and knowledge. Therefore, God is the source of all knowledge.

Trident: denotes three *Gunas* (qualities) with which God rules this world; *Satva* (calmness or goodness), *Rajas* (passion or motion) and *Tamas* (inertia).

Snakes around the neck: symbolizes death which means that God is immortal.

Garland of skulls: Reminds us of death which means man is mortal.

Three horizontal lines of ash on the forehead: Represent discipline, devotion and detachment (single-mindedness) that are necessary to achieve anything in life.

Third eye in the middle of the forehead: stands for wisdom or spiritual enlightenment. When Shiva opens his third eye this universe will be dissolved. The message is that the spiritual enlightenment destroys all evils.

Sitting on a tiger skin: the tiger represents the egoism in man's nature. The act of sitting denotes controlling egoism.

Resting one arm on the altar: control over selfishness.

Ganga entering His hair locks: Ganga represents the nectar of purity. We must acquire purity of mind.

MOTHER DURGA

'Durga' is a Sanskrit word which means fort, a metaphor for security or protection. God's function as protector of mankind is expressed in the female form, Mother Durga, symbolizing the earthly mother protecting her child during pregnancy and after birth. Mother Durga, worshipped as the *consort* of Shiva, is called by countless names and has numerous physical forms; some forms are very beautiful while others are quite grotesque. She is a benevolent looking mother to devotees, but can take the horrific form of Mother Kali to protect them from wicked forces. It would be outside the scope of this book to illustrate the countless varying forms of Durga and explain the metaphors attached to them. We will deal with her image which is most popular, especially in the north-west regions of India. Hindus from these regions have erected Durga temples in various parts of Canada, particularly in southern Ontario.

The most popular pose of Durga depicts her with a calm and smiling face, wearing a red dress, riding a lion. She is equipped with three eyes and eight arms, blessing devotees with one open hand and holding various objects in the other seven hands: conch shell, bow and arrows, thunderbolt, lotus, a disc revolving around her finger, sword, and trident. Let us examine the metaphor attached to each symbol.

Red dress: Red colour represents activity. According to a Puranic parable, she killed the male-buffalo-demon called Mahishasur and enraged him with her red dress. Buffalo represents all the negative forces and the red dress stands for activity. In other words, the demon of ego must be killed.

Lion: Lion is a metaphor for strength, determination and disciplined behavior. By riding a lion, Mother Durga is telling devotees to acquire mastery in such qualities if they want to destroy the demon of ego.

Eight arms: They represent eight directions i.e. east, west, north south, south-east, south-west, north-west, north-east. This means that Mother Durga protects us from all directions.

Three eyes: The left eye stands for desire, the right one represents action and the middle one is knowledge; these three qualities are essential in order to accomplish anything.

Conch Shell: It represents the sound produced by the word 'OM' symbolizing God in the form of word.

Bow & Arrows: Arrow is a metaphor for potential human energy. An arrow cannot be released without the help of a bow which converts the potential energy into force. The process of shooting the arrow to its target requires judgement and control. By holding the bow and arrow, Durga is telling her devotees to exercise judgement and control in utilizing their energies.

Thunderbolt: This is a symbol for firmness and strength. Here it means that Mother Durga's devotees must be firm in their convictions.

Lotus: As explained previously.

Revolving disc: As explained previously in Vishnu.

Sword: It denotes sharpness of intellect, ability to differentiate between good and evil.

Trident: As previously explained.

Blessing hand: This is a metaphor for assurance. Mother Durga is assuring her devotee freedom from fear.

GANESH

Ganesh, meaning Lord of the people, is worshipped by all Hindus in various parts of India. He is also called *Vinayaka*, the Supreme Leader, and *Vighneshwar* which means the Lord of Obstacles. All Hindu rituals start with first invoking Ganesha. Hindus worship him on all auspicious occasions and before starting any new venture. The artistic depiction of Lord Ganesh looks amusing or ridiculous to people who do not understand the art of God symbolism in Hinduism. He has an elephant head with a broken tusk, but the rest of his body is that of a human with a pot belly. He 'rides' a mouse. He has four hands and holds an object in each of them: a goad, a noose, a lotus and a bowl of rice balls. This apparently absurd characterization has a very logical explanation when we examine the significance of each feature.

Elephant head: The elephant represents wisdom. Large ears denote listening skills. One of the tusks is broken and this stands for imperfections.

Pot belly: It means an enormous appetite for spiritual

knowledge and wisdom.

Goad: It stands for control over mind.

Noose: It represents the controlling of sensual desires.

Lotus: A symbol of purity.

Bowl of rice balls: Sweetness or a reward.

Riding a mouse: Mouse represents ego and restless human mind. The act of sitting denotes controlling. It means that humility is acquired by controlling the ego, and peace by controlling the mind.

In this manner, Lord Ganesh offers us a formula for becoming a perfect human being: identify and remove your imperfections; acquire wisdom or spiritual knowledge by listening to spiritual masters; control your restless mind through meditation; harness your sensual desires; be pure in thoughts and action; be humble by controlling your ego. If we follow this formula, Lord Ganesh will reward us with the true sweetness of life.

The Carnival Of Chariots (The Rath Yatra) *[ref. pg 156]*

13.

SACRED MOTIFS, SYMBOLS & ARTICLES

During the early Vedic times, although various names were given to God's manifestations, Hindus did not worship God in ḥuman forms, nor did Vedas promote this idea. Giving forms to the formless God was a much later development. However, they did not suddenly switch from abstract concept to personification of God. In between the two, there was an intermediary stage when abstract motifs and emblems were developed to give forms to Formless, in an effort to describe the Indescribable. Outlined below are the three major abstract symbols which are still very popular with Hindus across the world, although not all Hindus may deploy them as mediums of ritualistic worship.

SACRED MOTIFS & SYMBOLS

OM: Om is the most significant symbol and expression in Hinduism. As a single-syllabled word, this is a symbol representing the Omnipresent God. Hindus use Om as an *incantation* or *Mantra* for meditation or chanting; all hymns used in performing ceremonies and rituals begin with Om.

The word *Om* is composed of three letters, namely A, U, and M, expressing Gods three main attributes: 'A' denotes His power to create; 'U' stands for his power to sustain and 'M' represents His power to dissolve the universe. As an abstract symbol, Om resembles the numeral 3, which again represents God's three attributes.

THE SWASTIKA: In the Sanskrit language, *Swastika* means 'good fortune', 'prosperity' or 'well-being', and thus symbolizes goodwill towards all human beings. The Swastika is an equilateral cross with its arms bent at right angle, all in the clock-wise direction. The right handed clock-wise Swastika is considered an auspicious solar symbol.

This is the most ancient and auspicious Hindu motif, but also sacred to Buddhists and Jains. For thousands of years, Hindus have been painting a Swastika on the each side of the main entrance of their homes. A swastika is also drawn on many objects used in worshipping and performing rituals. It has also been found on Greek coins, Celtic monuments, Byzantine buildings, and also in the burial grounds of some American Indians.

It is most unfortunate that the Swastika acquired notoriety in the Western world when Hitler used it as a Nazi symbol. Some people believe that the fall of Hitler was caused by his misuse of the Swastika power.

SHIVALINGA: The expression *Shivalinga* or *Sivalingam* is a combination of two Sanskrit words: Shiva Or Siva, a name given to God's power to dissolve and regenerate His creation, and Linga or Lingam meaning symbol, token, sign or gender. The Shivalinga looks like a short Cylindrical pillar with a rounded top projecting from a pedestal. The round shape connotes the message that God has no beginning and no end; He always existed when nothing was in existence, He will always exist when nothing will exist.

Hindus have used Shivalinga as an auspicious symbol and a medium for ritualistic worship of God for thousands of years. The ancient literature of Tamil Hindus refers to the setting up of ritual posts or altars, which probably pertains to Shivalinga. However, from the times the Western scholars started interpreting Hinduism, it became a centre of controversy as they described Shiva as a fertility god and the Linga as his phallus. Hindus are very much pained and offended by this vulgar distortion of their religious symbol. The overzealous Christian missionaries used this misinterpretation as a tool for anti-Hindu propaganda, in their efforts to convert uneducated Hindus to their faith. They condemned Hinduism as a primitive religion, and labelled Hindus as phallus

Some Hindu Symbols

OM *[ref. pg 143]*

Swastika

Tilka On Forehead

Bindi On Forehead

Durga

worshippers. Angered by this malicious and obscene propaganda, Mahatma Gandhi once commented, "It was in a Missionary (Christian) book that I first learned that Sivalinga has any obscenity at all..."

THE SACRED FIRE: All Hindu rites, including weddings, are performed around a fire, called Agni, created by burning small pieces of wood. Like the lamp, the light created by fire also denotes the victory of positive forces over evil ones. Since fire destroys the impurities of everything, it symbolizes purity. Fire also generate heat. Without heat or warmth, nothing can grow or exist on this earth. Therefore, fire is a metaphor for divine energy.

THE RISING SUN: All Hindu prayers and ceremonies are conducted while facing the east, for the sun rises from that direction. Many Hindus, as a form of worship, offer water to the rising sun every morning while saying a prayer. This ritual is also performed on many festivals and auspicious occasions. There are logical explanations for this symbolic act.

Like fire, the sun also represents the divine energy that sustains life on this earth through its heat and light. The significance of heat and light has already been explained above. But the sun also symbolizes certain aspects of Hindu philosophy. Sun rises in the morning, reaches its peak in the afternoon and sets in the evening; the next morning, it repeats the same cycle. This process represents the evolution of human life on earth- birth, growth and death. The sun also depicts the principle of life after death; the cycle which continues until the individual soul merges into the Supreme Soul. The sun also symbolizes punctuality and selfless acts.

OTHER SACRED OBJECTS AND ARTICLES:

In Hinduism, the art of symbolism is not limited to giving human or abstract form to God's attributes and powers. There are many other symbolic objects and articles that are considered sacred, for they are deployed in worshipping and performing rituals and ceremonies. Here, we will describe the significance of only a few major ones that are universally recognized by most Hindus.

THE CLAY LAMP: There is hardly any Hindu ceremony or ritual which is performed without first lighting a small lamp called *Diya or Deepak.* The lamp is made of a tiny round clay pot containing a cotton wick and oil. The light created by its flame removes the darkness. The light is a metaphor for all positive forces: truth, love, knowledge, spiritual wisdom and righteousness; darkness represents all negative forces such as ignorance, disease, poverty, hatred, prejudice, anger, violence, lust etc. Therefore, the lighting of a lamp symbolizes the destruction of evil things in life. Each component of the lamp also conveys a message. Since the clay pot is fragile and perishable, it represents the human body. The flame is the soul that dwells in the body. The human body is useless without the soul just as the lamp has no value without the flame. The oil symbolizes the human energy while the wick stands for the sense of sacrifice. Hence, the message is that hard work and sacrifice can overcome all obstacles.

THE COCONUT: The use of coconut, *Nariyal*, is very common in most Hindu rituals. When people set out on a important journey, a coconut is offered to them by their family. The host also gives a coconut to the guest when the latter departs. This is a very ancient Hindu tradition. This practice has both practical as well as metaphysical rationale.

From a practical point, the coconut is a very unique fruit; Unlike other fruits, it does not perish after ripening, and it also contains water inside the hard shell. In ancient times, when a journey was long and arduous, giving a coconut to a traveller made perfect sense as it provided both non-perishable food and water for the journey.

Being a fruit, the coconut is considered a symbol of prosperity and fertility. But it also has a much deeper spiritual significance. To reach the sweet water inside the coconut, one has to peel off the brown fibrous mesh and then crack the hard outer shell. The outer fibrous mesh of the coconut represents all negative human qualities; the hard shell represents ego, while the sweet water inside is a metaphor for spiritual enlightenment. In other words, attaining self-realization is a hard act to follow; one must shed all negative qualities and penetrate the fortress of ego.

There is also an historical explanation. In many primitive cultures, human sacrifice to appease the gods was common. Also, people were always willing to lay down their lives to protect their dignity, family and country. Since the coconut resembles a human skull, Hindus used it as a symbol of selfless-sacrifice, instead of following the practice of human sacrifice.

THE SACRED WATER POT: During the Hindu rituals and ceremonies, a round clay or metal pot, called *Kumbha or Kalush,* is worshipped. It is filled with water, decorated with religious motifs, and its mouth is covered with a coconut. At a practical level, a water pot placed near the sacred ceremonial fire serves the purpose of a fire extinguisher. However, as a sacred symbol, it has a spiritual significance. Fire represents heat and the water denotes coolness. The water pot reminds us that we must stay cool and calm in the face of tension generated by our activities to achieve our goals. It also carries another message: just as a pitcher without water is of no value, a life without a purpose is meaningless.

THE INCENSE: Hindus burn incense sticks and cones during their ceremonies. This practice is of both functional and moral value. As we all know, all types of aroma or smell are associated with a specific type of mood or environment. The sweet aroma of incense works as an air-freshener and creates an environment and mood for worship. Its fragrance also conveys a moral message: our presence and personality should emit positive thoughts and feelings. The incense stick has to burn itself for our benefit; similarly, we should bring joy to others even if we have to make personal sacrifices.

SANDALWOOD: At the outset of ceremonies, sandalwood paste is often applied to make a dot on the foreheads of those in attendance. When applied to the forehead, the sandalwood paste is considered to be very cooling. Its aroma and cooling effect promote a mood of prayer. Apart from this practical use, sandalwood is also associated with the principle of non-violence. When a sandalwood tree is cut down, its fragrance is so strong that it gets into the axe which strikes it. The message is that we must not be provoked to retaliate against those who hurt us; instead, like the sandalwood tree, we must exude kindness.

THE DOT ON THE FOREHEAD: Married Hindu women wear a round dot, called *Bindi,* in the centre of their foreheads. Traditionally, It is a symbol of chastity and purity. It serves the same purpose as the wedding band on the finger of a married woman in the western world. The dot on a married Hindu woman's forehead is a warning sign to men who may otherwise entertain unchaste thoughts about her. To many modern Hindu woman, it is just a beauty mark, and even single women and girls have started using it as a part of their make-up. In Canada, some Hindu women prefer not to wear a Bindi with western attire.

A dot in the middle of the forehead also has a spiritual connotation. It represents the *Third Inner Eye* which Hinduism encourages its adherents to awaken through Yoga and spiritual knowledge, in order to attain self-realization. That is why some men also wear a mark, called *Tilak* or *Tikka*, on their foreheads.

THE BELL: Most Hindu temples have a large overhead brass bell, *Ghunta*, suspended from the ceiling. People entering the temple ring the bell. The practical use of ringing the bell is to draw the temple-priest's attention to the devotee's presence, and enable him to come to the altar to offer his services to the latter. In the old days, when people did not have clocks and watches, the huge temple bell was rung to invite the people to attend public prayers. Similarly, a small bell, *Ghunti*, is also rung at the beginning of the prayer or a ceremony to let the congregation members know that the prayer has begun and they should observe complete silence. Spiritually, it symbolizes sound which is the language of devotion and love.

FRESH FLOWERS: No Hindu ritual or ceremony is performed without using fresh flowers. Flowers or garlands are offered to the deity; petals are showered to bless the host of the ceremony, a newly-wed couple or any other subject of the ceremony; special guests are also garlanded or showered with petals to welcome them. Using flowers on auspicious occasions is an excellent idea because of their two main attributes- beauty and pleasant fragrance. But, the beauty of flowers also symbolizes God's presence in nature, and His omnipresence.

PRASAD (OFFERINGS): Traditionally, Hindus bring sweets or fruits to the temple or to a ceremony as an offering to the deity. A small portion of it is symbolically offered to the deity while the rest is called *Prasad* or *Prasadam*, and is distributed among those in attendance. All Hindu ceremonies and prayer meetings conclude with the distribution of Prasad to the congregation. Anyone who visits a Hindu temple receives the Prasad from the priest after bowing or praying at the altar.

Literally, *Prasad* means kindness, blessing or favour. By making an offering to the deity, a Hindu symbolically acknowledges that whatever he has acquired in this world- food, wealth, knowledge or fame- is through the kindness and blessing of God; it all belongs to Him. The act of distributing the offering to the congregation denotes that whatever is left after meeting his own needs, will be used for the welfare of society.

VIBHUTI (SACRED ASHES): In many religious places in India, one can see holy men with their entire bodies smeared with white ashes which Hindus call *Vibhuti*, meaning Wealth. Some practising Hindus decorate their forehead with it. There are many other auspicious usages of *Vibhuti*. This seemingly 'primitive' ritual carries a deep spiritual message for Hindus. The Vibhuti is produced by ritually burning cow dung. From a practical viewpoint, the harmless smoke created by the burning of cow dung fumigates the environment. Symbolically, cow dung represents negative forces- lust, greed, hatred, anger, jealousy, ego, etc. Fire, representing spiritual wisdom, destroys all impurities and what comes out of it, the *Vibhuti*, is the wealth of purity. In other words, all negative forces can be destroyed by the fire of spiritual knowledge which gives us a wealth of purity in action and thoughts.

Many Hindus attach another significance to Vibhuti. Hindus cremate their dead bodies. Be it a king or a pauper, eventually, everyone turns into a pile of ashes. Therefore, the ashes as a symbol of human mortality remind the Hindus not to be egoist, and not to delay performing selfless deeds.

Some Hindu Symbols

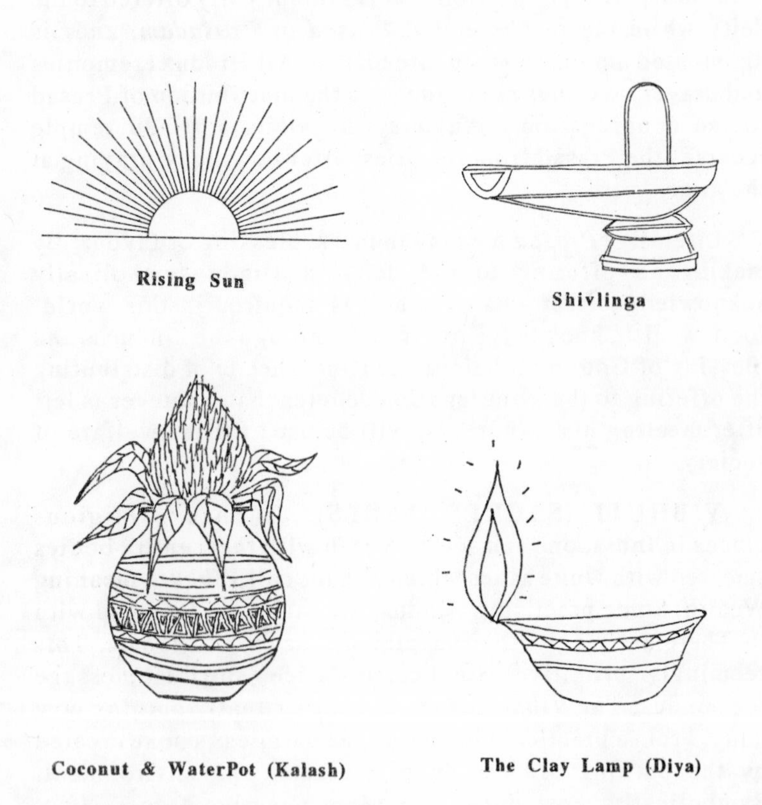

14.

HINDU WORSHIP, RITUALS AND RITES

MANY WAYS TO EXPRESS DEVOTION

To express intense love and stir emotions for God, a devotee needs a tangible focal point. A vast array of rituals, symbols, idols, and images of God representing His attributes fill this need in Hinduism. Although Christian Canadians may find this rich variety of channels that express devotion for God mind-boggling, but Hindus believe that any method or medium of worship will lead them to salvation, as long as it involves love, sincerity and devotion in following it. Once a devotee has fallen in love with God, every mode of expression is acceptable, however strange it may seem to others. Under the Bhakti (devotion) system, following devotional expressions are most commonly used although the detailed rituals may vary region to region.

POOJA: RITUALISTIC WORSHIP This is a Sanskrit word which means "to honour or worship". It is the most popular form of ritualistic worship Hindus have followed over the centuries. A Pooja involves an elaborate series of ritualistic 'offering' of goods, services and gestures of hospitality to honour one's favourite deity in the form of an idol. The deity is treated as an honoured 'guest'. The steps to perform a full and proper Pooja entail: invocation and praise, offering of water for washing and sipping, bathing the idol, offering a fresh garment, offering flowers and incense; waving a burning clay lamp in front of the deity, offering food, and at the end bidding farewell to the deity. After the conclusion the Pooja, food offered to the deity, called *Prasad*, is distributed among members of the family or the congregation because it is supposed to be blessed by the deity.

Many Canadian Hindus who practise their religion by following the Bhakti path set up a small shrine in a separate room or unused closet by adorning it with religious motifs, pictures or idols of their favourite deity or deities. Most of them do not know the elaborate procedure to perform a proper Pooja ordained by the scriptures, which is also very time consuming. Therefore, before leaving for work every morning, they would light a lamp and or an incense stick in front of the deity and stand with their hands folded and eyes shut, saying a short prayer. The extended Pooja is performed only on special occasions- e.g. birthday, house warming, children's graduation, some ancestor's death anniversary, promotion at work or some other happy occasion- by inviting to their homes a priest from the local temple or any lay-priest. This could be a private family Pooja or a public event attended by all friends and relatives. The event is usually followed by a sumptuous feast. For the sake of convenience, some Hindus organize the special Pooja at the local temple that can provide facilities to accommodate a large number of guests. It is worth mentioning here that, usually, Pooja and most Hindu ceremonies and rites are performed while sitting on the floor which symbolizes the display of humility. There are also practical aspects of this practice; usually, the performance is lengthy and therefore it would be very tiring to stand throughout the ceremony; people from India feel relaxed while sitting on the floor. However, most temples in Canada provide chairs, cushions and pillows for seniors or people with some medical problem.

KEERTAN: DEVOTIONAL MUSIC CONCERT: Hindus also express their love of God through music. Most public worships end with the singing of hymns or devotional songs, called *Bhajans*, with music. The members of the congregation clap and sing along swaying side to side with their eyes closed, and totally immersed in their love of God. To celebrate a special occasion, many Hindus organize a devotional music concert, called *Keertan*, either at their homes or at the temple. Most temples provide an amateur music group, called *Keertan Mundli* in Hindi language, with traditional musical instruments to give the performance. During the concert people offer donations, and the entire collection from the event goes to the temple or other charitable organizations. Many people bring traditional Indian sweets or fruits as offerings to the deity. In the end, all offerings are distributed as *Prasad* to those in attendance. In Canada, many temples also organize such devotional music concerts on a grand scale as a major public event for fund-raising. A Keertan can be a short concert lasting a few hours or an all night musical marathon, the *Jagrun*, with performances given by more than one music group.

YAJNA OR HAWAN, THE FIRE RITUAL: The Sanskrit Word *Yajna* has three meanings- *prayer to God, unification and religious giving or offering*. The full meaning of Yajna is to *perform selfless acts collectively*. This concept is symbolized by performing a 'fire ritual' which is also called Hawan. This ritual is performed in all religious rites and ceremonies of Hindus. It is believed that during the early Vedic period Hawan was the only ritualistic worship allowed by the scriptures, and the Pooja system is a much later development. Many scholars are of the opinion that Pooja was originally practised only by Dravidian natives but, later on, became a part of the Hindu worship system when their religious practices merged with the Vedic religion of Aryan settlers. The early Aryans used to perform the Hawans outdoors in the natural settings.

Like Pooja, a Hawan can either be a private family affair or a public event to mark or celebrate a special occasion. In many instances, both are combined, and the Pooja is followed by the Hawan or vice versa. The procedure involves making a small fire in a canister with an open top, called *Hawan Kund*. A special mixture of medicinal herbs, roots, dry fruits, sandal wood, incense and Ghee (clarified liquid butter), called *Samagree*, is used as offering. The whole procedure is directed and orchestrated by a priest. The Samagree and Ghee is poured into the fire, bit by bit, by the host and the other participants with the chanting of sacred verses (*Mantras*) from the Vedas. Each Mantra starts with the Om and ends with the expression *Swaha* (surrender). This act of putting Ghee and Samagree in the fire is called *Ahuti* or offering. Each Ahuti is then followed by the Mantra *Idam Na Mama* which means. *This is not mine or this is not being done for me*, signifying selfless sacrifice. The ceremony ends with the singing of devotional songs and distribution of Prasad and a feast. The host and guests also offer donations which usually go to the local temple or a charitable institution.

The Hawan or Yajna is not considered as worship of visible fire. It is only a symbolic act which denotes that all we possess is with God's grace and must be used for the benefit of the whole society. The Samagree represents the fruits of our labour and the act of pouring it in the fire means that what we produce is not sanctified unless we sacrifice a part of it for the benefit of others. Fire in Sanskrit is called *Agni* which is also a name for God. The spiritual significance of fire has already been explained elsewhere. The performance of Hawan also serves a practical purpose; the smoke and fragrance produced by the burning of herbal materials and incense, Samagree, fumigates and purifies the environment, which is especially beneficial in a tropical climate.

JAPA, THE SILENT REPETITION: *Japa* or *Japam*, meaning silent Repetition, is the practice of continuously repeating the God's name or a *Mantra*. Hindus who follow the emotional approach to worship God believe that constantly repeating His name or a Mantra, with utmost love and devotion, and without interruption, gives peace of mind, and purifies the soul. A similar practice was also adopted by the Russian Christian orthodoxy who tried to fulfill the biblical injunction to *Pray without ceasing*. Usually, a devotee would sit in a quiet place with his eyes shut and silently recite his favourite deity's name or a Mantra for an extended period of time, usually called Japa meditation. The most common recitations are: *Hare Rama, Hare Krishna, Om Namah Shivaya; Om Ganeshaya Namah*, etc. Some people use a rosary as an aid to Japa, and turn one bead each time the God's name is repeated. Some Hindus keep the Lord's name spinning amidst their daily activities- walking, shopping, working or driving, especially during the early morning hours.

BATHING IN THE HOLY GANGA : Hindus hold the river Ganga, called Ganges in the West, in utmost reverence, and affectionately call it *Mother Ganga* or *Goddess Ganga.* It originates from the Himalayas and flows through the plains of North-East regions of India. For centuries, Mother Ganga has been the subject of religious fables, folklores and poetry. Hindus literature refers to many sages and seers who composed their sacred verses or acquired divine enlightenment on the banks of Ganga. Since its water gives them prosperity by irrigating their land, Ganga is life-giving and thus considered sacred. It is also believed that the water of Ganga can be preserved for a long period of time without getting contaminated. Therefore, its water, called Ganga Jal, is also considered purifying, and used during most religious ceremonies. Every religious Hindu long for taking a dip in the Holy Ganga or *sitting in the lap of Mother Ganga,* believing that it would purify their body, mind and soul. When a Hindu is taking his last breath, the close family members pour a few drops of *Ganga Jal* (water) in his mouth as a last rite. When a Hindu Canadian is cremated, his ashes are taken to India and released with a ritual in the holy Ganga.

THE TEERTHA-YATRA: THE PILGRIMAGE: The Sanskrit word *Teertha* means a sacred abode, and *Yatra* means journey. The entire face of India is dotted with thousands of ancient temples and shrines of historical and religious significance. The most famous of all are the four major religious places, one in each direction: Jagannath Puri in the East (in the State of Orissa), Dwarika in the West (in the State of Gujarat), Badrinath in the North (in the State of Himachal Pradesh), and Rameshwaram in the South (in the State of Tamil Nadu).

In India, instead of going to holiday resorts, the traditional Hindus travel to the above listed places to pray and make offerings. When visiting India, Hindu Canadians also go on pilgrimages with their Canadian born children. Besides being a spiritual journey, there are also educational and social benefits of pilgrimage. Both children and adults learn the history of their traditions. Milling and rubbing shoulders with the people who share the same religious traditions and beliefs, although of diverse geographical or socio-economic background, generates a sense of unity, fraternity and broadens one's horizons. The tradition of going on a pilgrimage also helps Hindus remain attached to their religion.

THE RATH-YATRA: THE CARNIVAL OF CHARIOTS: The *Rath* is a chariot, and *Yatra* means journey. This is a sort of Hindus' Santa Claus parade or a religious *carnival of chariots*. On various special auspicious days, the local religious institutions and temples in different parts of India organize a procession to honour their favourite deities. The focal point of the parade is a huge brightly decorated traditional chariot carrying the idol of the local deity. The chariot, led by traditional musical bands, is manually pulled by hundreds of over-joyed devotees, and followed by thousands of people singing devotional songs and chanting hymns. In many cases, the procession ends at the banks of the nearest river or seaside where the clay image of the deity is ritually submerged into the water.

The Rath-Yatra of Lord Ganesh in Bombay, Goddess Kali in Calcutta and Lord Jagan Nath in Puri (Orissa) are amongst the most famous ones in India. This tradition is being kept alive in Canada by the followers of the Hare Krishna movement, who replicate the Rath-Yatra of Jagan Nath Puri in Toronto. This event usually takes place in the month of July or August each year. The Parade goes down Yonge Street towards Lake Ontario and ends at the Lakeshore, but the festivities and fair continues all day at Central Island.

THE FIVE DAILY DUTIES

The ancient Hindu sages realized that it was easy to believe in the lofty ideal of self-sacrifice, but it would be difficult for ordinary people to apply it in their daily lives. To help people practise self-sacrifice everyday, Manu, the ancient Hindu writer on ethics, prescribed five daily obligations, *Panchmaha Yajna*, for householders:

1. **Brahma Yajna-** Sacrifice to the holy scriptures
2. **Deva yajna-** Sacrifice to God
3. **Pitri Yajna-** Sacrifice to parents

4. Purusa Yajna- Sacrifice to people
5. Bhoota Yajna- Sacrifice to creatures

Before we describe each of the five daily obligations in detail, it must be emphasized that they have both external and internal application, and the medium for the external application may vary from region to region or from sect to sect.

Brahma Yajna: Sacrifice to the Holy Scriptures

Brahma is the name for God's creative attribute. According to Hindu belief, when God created this world (in addition to material things to sustain life on this earth) he gave knowledge and spiritual wisdom to help people conduct their lives virtuously, and attain salvation; such divine knowledge is contained in the four Vedas. Therefore, it is the duty of every Hindu to study and teach the spiritual wisdom contained in their holy scriptures. Since Vedas are in pre-classic Sanskrit, it is impossible for the average person to read or comprehend them. On account of this practical difficulty, they read various other sacred books (e.g. Gita, Ramayana or Upanishads) which have been translated into many Indian and foreign languages, including English. Those who cannot read can listen to discourses given by other learned people, or have someone read it to them; usually, illiterate elders have their children or grandchildren read a holy book to them.

After the self-study, Hindus must pass on or propagate the knowledge they have acquired. However, many who do not have the skill or aptitude to do so, offer assistance in many practical ways to individuals and institutions that propagate the spiritual wisdom. For example, Canadian Hindus discharge this obligation by sponsoring a religious radio or TV program or organizing or financing a public discourse by a holy man visiting from India. Some Hindus hold a scripture reading session, called *Paath*, in their homes and invite friends and relatives to attend it. It is important to know that studying and spreading the sacred knowledge is not considered fruitful unless it is applied internally.

Deva Yajna: Sacrifice to God: The sacrifice to God is done in the form of a Hawan which has already been described in this chapter. In modern times, it is not possible to perform the Hawan every day since this is a time consuming exercise. Therefore, it has been replaced with other forms of worship and prayer.

Pitri Yajna: Sacrifice to Parents & Ancestors:

The word *Pitri* means parents and ancestors. After God, we owe our existence to our parents and ancestors. Our parents brought us into this world, nurtured us, gave us all necessities of life and education. Therefore, the Hindu scriptures say that the mother and father are worthy of reverence. The grandparents and other ancestors are also equally important as they created things which we now enjoy. In Hindu families, the younger members are expected to display utmost courtesy and politeness towards their elders. In traditional families, such reverence is externally expressed by touching their feet, an act which denotes utmost humility. This practice is no longer common among Hindu Canadians.

It is the moral obligation of Hindus to take care of their retired or disabled parents and grandparents; they must sacrifice to ensure that their elders' physical and emotional needs are adequately met. In Hindu society, people who neglect their parents and elders are looked down upon. Hindus also express their gratitude towards the dead ancestors by performing an annual ritual called *Shraddha* which literally means faith and devotion. This tradition is a Thanksgiving day and Remembrance day combined into one. Each year, on the death anniversary of their parents or grandparents, divout Hindus invite a Brahmin (male or a female, depending on the gender of the deceased ancestor) to their homes for a feast. The invited guest is honoured as a substitute for their dead ancestor, and treated with specially prepared food, and gifts. Of course, the food and gifts given to the Brahmin guest do not reach the dead ancestor, but, this custom does give Hindus a formal opportunity to express their love and gratitude for the deceased ancestors. Some Hindus, instead of inviting a

Brahmin guest, offer food to the needy and poor or donate money to their favorite charitable society in the memory of the deceased ancestor. Many Hindu Canadians follow the Shraddha custom by delivering groceries to their local food bank.

Purusa Yajna: Sacrifice to People

The concept of serving mankind is embodied in this obligation of sacrifice which is discharged through the rendering of genuine hospitality to all guests or visitors, and by feeding the hungry and sheltering the homeless. Hindus are known for treating even a casual visitor to their home with generosity. In the olden days, Hindu families offered food and shelter to wandering holy men whose presence was considered sanctifying. In modern times, Hindus give money or clothes to beggars and destitute. In Canada, Hindus meet this obligation by donating money to charities or delivering groceries to the nearest food bank.

Bhoota Yajna: Sacrifice to Creatures

The term *Bhoota* refers to all living beings besides humans. Since all living things are created by God, Hindus are duty bound to feed, protect and show consideration to members of the animal kingdom, especially those who are helpful to human beings. It means taking good care of farm and domestic animals or pets. Traditional Hindus, especially older people, discharge this duty daily by putting aside some food from their dinner plate before they start eating. The parted portion of the dinner is then fed to a domestic animal or put outside the house for birds or vagrant pets and animals. Many Hindus make donations to animal shelters run by charitable organizations.

The object of these five daily duties prescribed to Hindus is to remind them everyday that each individual is an integral part of the world around him, and his prosperity and progress depends on the welfare of others, including birds and animals.

THE SIXTEEN SANSKARAS (SACRAMENTS)

Like other religions, Hindus are also prescribed a number of ceremonies called *Sanskaras,* also pronounced *Samskaras*, which means the actions which purify, refine or reform. The nearest English translation is Sacraments. When a diamond is found in a mine, it does not look beautiful until it is refined and polished. Similarly, a human being must also undergo some purifying ceremonies in order to shine spiritually. In Hinduism, the Sanskaras are not superstitious acts to ward off evil spirits; their objective is to invoke favourable results, and to allow Hindus to express their joys and sorrows, hopes and ambitions in a dignified manner. Like the traffic signs on the highways, the Sanskaras also give directions to human life at every crucial stage of its development, starting from conception and ending at death. The sage Angiras poetically compares the Sanskaras to a painting:

> "Just as a picture is painted with various colours, so the character of the individual is formed by the proper performance of the Samskaras."

According to Max Muller, these ancient ceremonies reveal "the deep rooted tendency in the heart of man to bring the chief events of human life into contact with a higher power, and give to our pure joys and sufferings a deeper significance and a religious sanctification."

Hindus have sixteen Sanskaras but most people no longer perform each and every of them. Therefore, we will describe all of them briefly, but elaborate on only the most important ones.

1. Garbhadan: This ceremony is performed when a married couple decides to have a child. According to Hindu scriptures, even the act of a man to approach his wife for sexual intercourse to procreate is a sacred duty. Blessings and prayers are offered ritually for a virtuous and healthy child.

2. Punsavana: Three or four months after conception, this Sanskara is performed by the parents for the sound growth of the child in the embryonic stage. During the ritual, they pray for the birth of a worthy and physically healthy child, and a few drops of the juice of the banyan tree stem is poured into the pregnant woman's nostrils. According to Hindu medical science, *Ayurveda,* the banyan tree extract is beneficial during pregnancy.

3. Simantonnayana: In this third pre-natal Sanskara, performed between five and eight months of pregnancy, certain rituals are aimed at keeping the would-be mother in a happy mood. Prayers are also offered for full and proper development of a child's organs.

4. Jatakarma: The child is formally welcomed into the new world with this sanskara.

5. Namakarna: This is the name-giving ceremony that takes place on the 11th day after birth. Hindus attach great significance to the name. The name chosen for the child is supposed to be a source of inspiration. It is quite common to name the child after great sages, heroes and kings or other famous historical and mythological characters. Most Hindu names are meaningful. In many instances, the first syllable of the name is based on the science of numerology or astrology.

6. Nishkramana: After keeping the child indoors for four months, the child is taken outdoors to be introduced to nature. The child is exposed to the sun rays with a prayer for a long life.

7. Annaprashana: During the first six to eight months, the child is breast-fed. When teeth begin to appear, the first feeding of the child with solid food is an important event in the child's growth. This stage is sanctified with prayers and rituals. This Sanskara is widely practised amongst the Bengali community in Canada.

8. Choodakarma: This is the head-shaving ceremony, usually performed during the first to third year. During the ceremony, a prayer is uttered for the good health and intellectual development of the child. According to Hindu medical science, shaving of the head after birth promotes healthy hair growth and enhances brain power. Charaka, the famous Hindu medical scientist of the ancient times, was of the opinion that cutting and dressing of hair, clipping of nails and trimming of the beard gave vigour, purity and beauty.

9. Karnavedha: This Sanskara takes place at the age of three years when the child's ears are ritually pierced with prayers for good health. It is believed that the purpose of this ancient practice was both medical and ornamental. The piercing of ears for wearing jewellery, by males and females, was quite common in most ancient civilizations. This custom has also reappeared in North America. Medically, it is considered an acupuncture to prevent hernia.

10. Upanayana: This word means to *acquire sight* that can *see within*. In the ancient times, this Sanskara was usually performed from age five to eight years when a child was formally placed in the care of a Guru for spiritual education. Like the *Confirmation* in Christianity and *Bar-Mitzvah* in Judaism, Upanayana is an important landmark in the life of a Hindu. In Vedic times, both boys and girls underwent this rite, but as the status of women went down, girls were no longer entitled to it.

This ceremony is also called *Yajnopaveet*, or the *sacred thread ceremony*. After a Hawan is performed, the boy is given a large circular sacred thread consisting of three strands. The three strands symbolize the three aspects of God i.e. *Creator, Sustainer and Regenerator*. Some believe they represent three virtues- knowledge, action and devotion. The sacred thread hangs loose diagonally from the left shoulder across the right hip. The boy takes the vow of celibacy, Brahmacharya, which is of great importance in the life of a Hindu student. The thread reminds him of his vow. From this stage, his status is upgraded to that of a Dvija or twice born because he starts a new life of learning to acquire knowledge. The ceremony ends with a feast.

11. Vidyarmbha: This expression literally means the beginning of education. The ceremony is performed immediately after Upanayana, in order to formally introduce a child to the alphabet. He offers prayers to Ganesh, the deity of auspiciousness and *Saraswati,* the deity of knowledge and art.

12. Samavartana: This Sanskara, performed between twenty-first to twenty-fifth year, marks the completion of education. It is like the modern day convocation or graduation function. The young Hindu is now considered ready to be employed and participate in the social and economic life of the community. This ceremony is very popular among Hindu Canadians.

13. Vivaha (Wedding): The Wedding ceremony, called *Vivaha Sanskara*, which literally means *to carry with the best of abilities*, is prescribed for the purpose of sanctifying the marriage. The process of marriage used to be a very elaborate one, full of numerous colourful rituals spread over a period of two weeks and ending with the actual wedding ceremony. Gradually, the demands of modern life made it a much shorter affair. Busy Hindu Canadians cut it down to a one day event. For the interest of the readers, instead of limiting ourselves to the actual wedding rituals, we are describing below a typical North Indian Hindu wedding in its entirety.

THE WEDDING CEREMONY & VOWS:

Wedding, a family affair: The entire Hindu family participates actively and enthusiastically in organizing the wedding of one of its members; each member has a key role to play. Many relatives from India and other provinces of Canada also arrive to attend the wedding. The parents usually spearhead the whole operation in active consultation with the bride or the groom. The parents from both sides hold a series of meeting to plan the wedding. Modern Canadian Hindus have broken and modified many centuries old customs in order to integrate the wedding ceremony into the social environment of their adopted land.

In India, the actual wedding ceremony is always held at the residence of the bride's parents who are responsible for the entire cost of the ceremony including reception. The groom arrives at the bride's house in the form of a procession called Baraat. The colourful process is headed by a series of live bands, and the groom rides a beautifully ornamented horse. The procession ends at the bride's residence where the groom's wedding party is formally received by her parents, relatives and guests. In Canada, the same process takes place but in a improvised manner. Here, the wedding either takes place in a temple or a community hall followed by a reception, usually a gala extravaganza. Many affluent Hindus arrange the entire event in a five or star hotel and the cost is shared by both sides. After buying a house, the wedding of a son or a daughter is the second major expense in an average Hindu family.

The wedding ceremony is held under a colourful canopy, called Mundup or Vedi, adorned with fresh or silk flower festoons and glittering lights, set up in the wedding hall. The main entrance or the gate of the wedding hall or hotel is also decorated with festoons. The groom's family, friends and guests assemble near the wedding hall, usually the parking lot, and form a wedding procession which is led by some sort of music arrangement, drummers, or large *ghetto-blasters*. In Punjabi Hindu weddings, the young men and women dance to the music boisterously in front of the wedding procession to give a carnival or parade flair to the event. The groom's wedding party is received at the entrance by the hosts, the bride's family and relatives. The colourfully dressed and adorned bride, escorted by wedding maids, slowly and gracefully walks to the entrance to formally welcome the groom. While the priest chants the *Mantras*, she puts a large garland, specially prepared for the occasion, around the groom's neck. The groom gracefully bows to receive the garland, the bashful bride gives him a repressed smile and the audience of guests and hosts clap. This is a very touching moment cherished by the couple. The guests in the grooms party are greeted with a garland, bouquet or a flower as a gesture of honour and friendship. They are offered soft drinks and light snacks.

The next step is called *Milani* or greeting. Each close relative of the bride garlands and embraces the respective relative of the groom. For instance, the bride's father greets the groom's father, her brother greets his brother, her uncles greet his uncles, so on and so forth. They are formally introduced to each other. After a brief interlude, the guests on both sides settle down in chairs laid around the wedding canopy to witness the wedding ceremony. The parents from both sides, the priest arranged by the bride's parents, and the groom sit on the floor cross-legged under the canopy, waiting for the bride to arrive. The ceremony commences after the bride walks slowly to the *Mundup*, escorted by her maternal uncle, followed by close female relatives and friends.

The wedding ceremony, usually one to two hours long, consists of a series of symbolic rituals performed in front of a fire lit in a small steel cannister, called *Hawan Kund*, with small pieces of wood and camphor. The rituals may slightly vary according to the region of India the bride's family come from. Most Hindu rites are performed in front of a fire which symbolizes purity and represents all other divine attributes. The major rituals of the wedding ceremony are as follows:

Pani grahan or Kanyadan: The bride's father places her right hand in the groom's hand and declares to the assembly that he is giving away his daughter who has agreed to marry the groom of her own free will. The bride's mother also gives her approval by pouring the sacred water on their joined hands. The priest then helps the bride and the groom light the sacred fire and perform the ***Sacrifice*** rite. As the priest recites the Vedic hymns, they make offerings into the fire and place their faith in the omnipresent God.

Lajahuti and Satpadi: The corner of the bride's Saree or dress is tied into a knot with the end of the groom's waistband which denotes union. The bride's brothers stand beside her to give her parched rice which she offers to the fire. They both slowly walk around the sacred fire four times; the bride leads in the first three rounds and the groom in the last one. The couple then take seven steps together while the priest recites the hymns with each step explaining their duties as householders. They both sit down and the groom invites the bride to exchange her seat and sit on his left i.e. close to his heart where she now belongs. The priest makes seven statements on her behalf before she accepts his invitation:

1. *We are both lucky to meet each other, and thank God for that.*

2. *I want your love, not just gifts to please me.*
3. *I shall be your true partner for life, and hereafter I will join you in all endeavors.*
4. *I will stand by you in good and bad times.*
5. *I should be accepted by your relatives and they too should invite me along with you, otherwise I will not go with you uninvited.*
6. *I shall accept your family with great pleasure. You have to accept my family the same way.*
7. *When you are out of town on business, you are not to spend time with other women.*

The groom responds by making the following statement:

> *"These vows are difficult. I am a human being and may err, but I make this promise by touching your head and keeping my hand towards your heart: From today and onward your heart is mine and my heart is yours; I bind your mind and heart with this promise; Once our hearts are united these conditions are not necessary."*

After some more rituals, the guests and relatives gather around the newly wed couple and give them their blessings, *Ashirvad*, showering them with flower petals. The assembly adjourns until the reception time in the evening.

If the bride or the groom is a non-Hindu, the Hindu parents usually agree to a second wedding ceremony according to his or her faith. This shows the tolerance and respect Hindus have for other faiths.

14. Vanaprastha: Having completed the first two stages of life, being a student and a householder, a Hindu enters the retirement stage with this ceremony in preparation for the next stage of total detachment. This rite is not commonly performed by Canadian Hindus.

15. Sanyasa: This ceremony marks the beginning of the last phase of life when a Hindu renounces all worldly attachments and directs all his activities towards God.

16. Antyesthi: This is the funeral rite connected with cremation. Hindus cremate the body, symbolizing that all five elements of the body - namely, earth, water, fire, air and ether-merge back with these elements in nature. Traditionally, a funeral pyre is prepared with firewood to cremate the body. Prayers are offered for peace to the departed soul, and the officiating priest gives comfort to the bereaved family by quoting from the scriptures and reinforcing the concept of immortality of the soul. Usually, the eldest son of the deceased performs all the rituals guided by the priest, and torches the funeral pyre. In Canada, instead of the funeral pyre, Hindus use the modern system of cremation. The ashes and the remains are taken to India by the eldest son or the closest family member and released in the holy Ganga (Ganges) with another ritual.

Hindus usually wear white clothes, symbol of purity, at the funeral, and sit on the floor, which symbolizes humility, while visiting the family of the deceased to offer condolences. Mourning lasts for twelve days and a formal public ceremony, consisting of Hawan and prayers, is performed at the house of the deceased on the thirteenth day to end the mourning period. The actual procedure of the ceremony may vary from region to region. In North India, the priest wraps a turban around the head of the heir, usually the eldest son. The purpose of the *Pugree* (turban) ceremony is to formally and publicly declare him the heir and new head of the household. To express respect for the deceased and allow the family to overcome their grief, most Hindu families refrain from celebrating any happy events, weddings, birthdays and festivals for twelve months after the death. The first death anniversary is marked by the formal ceremony of Hawan and prayers, attended by all relatives and friends of the deceased.

THE PRACTICE OF *SUTTEE* (self immolation)

This is not a Hindu rite, ritual or custom, but many people in the western world seem to think it is. We are, therefore, dissussing this issue in order to alleviate this misconception.

In every culture, man has inflicted the most horrible cruelty on his fellow beings in the name of religion, although such acts may be a total affront to his religion itself. The practice of *Suttee*, known as Widow burning to the sensational Western media, in the Hindu society of the Middle Ages belonged to such a category of social evils.

The origin of the *Suttee* practice lies in a Hindu woman's intense love for her deceased husband being taken to an extreme. In the Hindu society, marriage was, and still is, considered a permanent union of two souls, and the relationship of the wife and husband is typically described as one soul in two bodies. In some cases, a women would be so distraught by her beloved husband's sudden and untimely death that she considered her life totally worthless without him. Under the extreme pressure of emotional stress, the grieving widow would commit the act of self-immolation, willingly, by ritually sitting on her husband's funeral pyre in the presence of a priest. Sometimes, the greedy relatives, who were to inherit the deceased couple's property, conspired with the village priest and provoked her to do so. Over the centuries, many myths, fables and folklores developed around the practice of *Suttee*. Some people claimed that such a woman experienced no pain during the act of *Suttee*. In any event, Suttee has never been a common or standard practice among widows at any time in India. On the few occasions it occurred, it was mostly in the region of Rajasthan, the land of Rajpoot warriors, known for their legendary valour. After their husbands died in the battlefield, the wives committed suicide *en masse* by jumping in a specially prepared pyre, in order to protect their chastity from foreign invaders

In Hinduism, human life is the best and the most precious creation of God, and must be preserved. It heavily emphasizes non-violence, *Ahinsa*, and promotes animal protection. It is unthinkable that such a religion would sanction or condone suicide for any reason whatsoever. On the contrary, Hindu social reformers and religious leaders of all times condemned the *Suttee* practice and worked for its abolition. Finally, Raja Ram Mohan Roy, the great social reformer of the 19th century, agitated aggressively against this inhumane practice and compelled the British rulers to legally ban it. In modern India, committing or encouraging someone to commit the act

Private Worship (Pooja) At Home *[ref. pg 151]*

7. **The Wedding Ceremony** *[ref. pg. 164]*

Devotional Music Concert (Keertan) In Temple *[ref. pg 152]*

The Fire Rituals (Hawan) *[ref. pg 153]*

Lord Krishna Counselling Dejected Warrior *Arjuna* In The Battlefield Of "Mahabharata."

Sister Tying *Rakhi* On Brother's Wrist On "Rakshabandhan" Festival *[ref. pg 180]*

Children Celeberating "The Holi" Festival *[ref. pg 171]*

of *Suttee* is still a serious crime. However, some isolated incidents do occur in the remote and socially backward areas every few years. Such incidents are so heavily over-played and sensationalized by the media that one tends to get the impression that Hindu widows commit *Suttee* routinely.

Bathing In Holy Ganga *[ref. pg.154]*

15.

MAJOR FESTIVALS

Hinduism is well known for its colourful festivals. Like rituals and rites, they have kept Hindus attached to their religion for thousands of years. Most festivals are so ancient that it would be difficult to trace their origin. There are regional and universal festivals, and the same festival may be celebrated in a different way and for a different reason in various regions of India even though the central theme may be the same. It would be beyond the scope of this book to talk about each and every Hindu festival; we shall, therefore, limit ourselves only to the major ones.

Basically, there are three types of Hindu festivals: **religious**, directly linked with Hinduism; **social**, celebrating human relationships, birthdays of great heroes and personalities, historical or mythological, and anniversaries of certain important events; **seasonal**, welcoming the arrival of each new season that brings new hopes, happiness and colours. Regardless of the reasons or origin, all festivals involve some form of worship, wearing of new clothes and feasting; however, any type of merrymaking must not include the use of liquor or non-vegetarian food.

FESTIVALS AND CALENDAR:

Most Hindu Canadians have forgotten their Hindu calendar since India still uses the English calendar for schools and offices, introduced by the British. However, Hindu festivals are observed on the dates of the Hindu Calendar based on lunar cycle, and do not fall on the same dates of the English calendar each year. Therefore, it is important to become acquainted with the Hindu Calendar, called *Panchang*.

The time taken by the earth, slightly over 365 days, to circle the sun is the solar year on which the English calendar is based. However, the Hindu calendar is based on the movement of the moon around the earth, and the lunar year is comprised of 354 days. In order to reconcile the two, an extra month is added to the Hindu calendar every third year which contains 13 months.

The Hindu year has twelve months: *Chaitra, Vaishakha, Jyeshtha, Ashadha, Shravana, Bhadraprada, Ashwina, Kartika, Margshirsha, Pausha, Magha and Phalguna.* There are thirty days in each month which is divided into two fortnights called *Paksha.* The fifteen days when the moon is gradually increasing are called *Shukla Paksha.* The next fifteen days when the moon decreases are known as *Krishna Paksha.* Each month starts with a new moon.

HOLI, THE FESTIVAL OF COLOURS

Holi is a festival of joy, gaiety and merry-making. In the modern context, Holi is a carnival, Thanksgiving day, New Year Eve, the Calgary Stampede, first April Fools Day, and Halloween, all rolled into one. Holi is celebrated in March (Phalgun in Hindu Calendar) to mark the arrival of the spring which brings colours, and also represents the spirit of youthful vigour and vitality. People are happy that the winter is over. The farmers are joyous to see their crops ready for harvest.

Apart from welcoming the spring, Holi is celebrated for different reasons and called with different names in various regions of India. In Northern India, it is believed that the word Holi is derived from *Holika*, a female demon and one of the characters of a mythological story. The story is about the conflict between a demonic and atheist king, Hirnakashyap, and his son Prahalad who was a staunch devotee of God. Hirnakashyap wanted his people to worship him instead of God, and tortured those who refused to do so. When his own son defied him, Hirnakashyap tortured him and arranged many *accidents* to have him killed, but Prahalad miraculously survived each time. Hirnakashyap hatched another conspiracy with his sister Holika to kill him. Holika had the boon of being indestructible by fire. She sat on a pyre and persuaded Prahalad to sit in her lap. To everyone's surprize, Holika was burnt to death but Prahalad came out unhurt and alive. The over-joyed followers of Prahalad went berserk. They pushed, shoved and lifted each other, and in a mood of sheer frenzy they started a mock fight throwing sand, water, mud or whatever else they could lay their hands on. The riotous crowd ran amuck in the streets shouting "Holika is dead." According to another legend, Holi was celebrated to mark the slaying of a female demon Putna by baby Krishna when she attempted to murder him. In both cases, the central theme of Holi is the victory of good over evil.

The celebration starts one night before the Holi when the boisterous groups of boys go around the streets gathering wood that includes old furniture people throw away after spring cleaning. The collected fuel is piled high in the centre of the village square to create a bonfire. Before the fire is lit, the women perform rituals and offer prayers while circling around the pile. People sing and dance around the bonfire accompanied by drums and cymbals, while noisy youths make merry and play practical jokes on each other.

The next day is the Holi or Phag day (derived from the name of month Phalgun) when the spirit of goodwill and friendship breaks all barriers and disparities. Holi turns enmity into amity; old enemies forgive each other, shake hands and become friends again. People of all ages, castes, economic or social status abandon their differences, shed all inhibitions and go wild with an ecstasy of merry-making. Adults go door to door boisterously exchanging greetings and sharing homemade sweets with everybody in the neighborhood. They put garlands of fresh flowers around each other's necks and embrace each other joyously. People amuse themselves by splashing each other with coloured water and throwing coloured powder, called Gulal or Abeer, on each other while chanting "This is Holi. This is Holi." Boys recreate the frenzied aftermath scene of Holika's destruction by running amuck in the streets, playing pranks, clowning around, breaking into mock fights, shouting and screaming. The chaotic and riotous celebrations end in the afternoon when everyone goes home to wash and clean. The fun and frolic resume in the evening in a more orderly manner. Entertainment during the evening ranges from the reciting of raunchy jokes and poems to sophisticated cultural events such as poetry recitals and plays. Some city folks organize an amateur public comedy show called *Maha Moorakh Sammelan* or *the Convention of great fools*. The performers are, usually, politicians and other prominent persons of the city. They recite comic poetry, tell jokes and select The Greatest Fool who is roasted' with friendly insults, offered booby prizes and a large garland of old shoes.

Apart from its spiritual and social aspects, Holi is an annual mass *psycho-therapy* which allows Hindus an outlet for the release of their pent up emotions. The Holi spirit turns even the most serious and stern adults into jokers, clowns and pranksters, all without the use of alcohol.

RAM NAVAMI

This is the birthday of Lord Rama (Hindus pronounce it as Ram) which Hindus celebrate in March or April (Chaitra in Hindu Calendar). The word *Navami* refers to the 9th day of the Shukla Paksha. Rama was born in the famous Raghu dynasty of kings in the city of Ayodhya. Currently, his birth place is a hot political issue in India causing riots between Hindus and Muslims. It is believed that in the year 1528 A.D the Muslim zealots demolished the temple which stood on the site where Rama was born, and erected a Mosque on its site. Some Hindu organizations, supported by a political party, want to reconstruct the temple. The year of Rama's birth has also fueled a fierce debate among historians, scholars and Hindu theologians. Some believe he was born in the 8th century B.C. while others push the time of his birth to long before 3000 B.C. This subject is beyond the scope of this work. However, the story of Rama briefly narrated in another chapter is called *Ramayana* meaning *The ways of Rama.*

Most Hindus worship Rama as the 7th incarnation of God while many adore him as a great God-like personality. However, all Hindus revere Rama as a personification of all that is good and great in human character. He represents every conceivable ideal in the human behaviour. He is an embodiment of the most perfect human values and familial relationships. He was not only a model king and a brave warrior, but also an ideal friend, husband, brother and son. For centuries, Rama's name has echoed streets, homes and temples in India as Hindus believe that even repeating his name alone purifies the soul. The idols and pictures of Lord Rama adorn Hindu homes and temples around the world. Hindus name their children after Rama hoping it will encourage them to be like him. A Hindu who is devoid of good character or behaviour is often told, "There is no Ram in you."

On the Ram Navami day, Hindus worship Rama at home and visit the local temple. Like Christmas, this is the day for family get together and feasting. The temples in Canada organize special programs of devotional music, drama and the recital of Ramayana. The festival of Ram Navami is a reminder to Hindus that they should imbibe some of the ideals Rama represents. Considering the rapid erosion of traditional moral and family values, the legacy of Rama is more relevant today than ever before.

SHIVARATRI

The word *Shivaratri*, translated as *The Night of Shiva*, is made up of two words- Shiva, the regenerating aspect of God, and Ratri which means night. It falls during the dark fortnight, *Krishna Paksha*, of Phalguna (February/March). It is considered to be the night festival for the devotees of Shiva. They observe a 24-hour fast and keep a strict vigil overnight meditating, chanting, singing devotional songs and reading literature extoling the glory of Lord Shiva. The *Lingam*, the symbol of Shiva, is worshipped by offering Ganges water, curd, milk, fruits, flowers, bael leaves, honey and liquid butter (Ghee). The exact method of worshipping varies from one region to another.

Since Shivaratri is a very ancient festival, there are many legends and stories about its origin and significance. According to one mythological explanation, on this day, the devotees of Shiva celebrate the *marriage* of Shiva and his *consort* Parvati. It is also connected with a story of how a hunter, called Suswar, acquired the grace of Lord Shiva when he unintentionally worshipped him. The story goes that one day when Suswar was being chased by a hungry tiger, he climbed up a tree to save his life. The frightened hunter stayed up the tree all night as the tiger sat under the tree waiting for his meal to come down. Suswar, hungry and thirsty, started plucking and throwing down the leaves just to keep himself awake. It so happened that the leaves were falling on the top of a Shiva Lingam located under the tree. Lord Shiva was very pleased with his worship, though done unintentionally, and blessed him. In his next life, Suswar was reborn as a king named Chitrabhanu who observed Shivaratri with his people.

Followers of the modern Arya Samaj movement link Shivaratri with their founder, Swami Dayanand, whose boyhood experience inspired him to seek the truth about God on this day. On the night of Shivaratri, when the boy Moolshankar (Swami Dayanand's real name) stayed awake observing the fast, he noticed a rat climbing the Shiva Lingam and eating the offerings of food. He started wondering why people worshipped the God who could not even protect Himself from a rat. This question set Moolshankar on the course of searching for the true knowledge of God. His study, research and interpretation of the Vedas transformed him into Swami Dayanand.

However, according to many Hindus, Shivaratri has a deep philosophical significance which lies in the literal meaning of the expression Shivaratri, a combination of two words- *Shiva* and *Ratri*. The word *Shiva* is made up of two syllables- *Shi* and *va*. Shi denotes 'removal of sins', and va means 'release from worldly ties'. In other words, *Shiva* symbolically represents the fatherly aspect of the Omnipotent and Omnipresent God who helps us keep away from sinful acts which will result in attaining Moksha, the release from the cycle of births and deaths. The word Ratri is also a combination of two syllables- Ra which means pain and miseries, and tri connotes remover or destroyer. Symbolically, Ratri denotes the motherly aspect of God, for a child forgets all the stresses and strains when he peacefully sleeps in the lap of his mother. Thus, the festival of Shivaratri celebrates the union of the fatherly and motherly aspects of God.

Regardless of its origin, Shivaratri reinforces Hindus' faith in the greatness and glory of God. The act of fasting makes them experience themselves the pangs of hunger that starving people around the world suffer. It also offers them an opportunity to spend a night with their family, which helps them to retain their spiritual heritage.

NAVARATRI/DURGA POOJA

The word *Navaratri* is composed of two words- *Nava* and *Ratri*. Literally, *Nava* means nine and *Ratri* means night. It is also called Durga Pooja as the devotees of Mother Durga worship her and observe fasting for nine days. This festival is celebrated twice a year, once in Chaitra (March/April) and again in Ashwina (September/October). Some Hindu scholars offer two reasons for celebrating it twice.

Firstly, another name for the Supreme Energy is *Shakti* which literally means energy or power. Shakti symbolizes the Divine Energy that moves all the planets in order to maintain them in the universe in the correct balance. Navaratri offers Hindus an opportunity to thank the Divine Energy for this important task. Secondly, Hindus believe that the potent energy released by the movements of planets influences the development of the human mind and body. During the Navaratri days, Hindus pray to God to endow them with this energy to maintain their physical and mental balance.

Navaratri is observed for nine days and nine nights. The nine days and nights are divided into three sets of three days and nights, and each set is devoted to worshipping three different aspects of God, the Supreme Energy: the first set to Mother Durga, the second to Lakshmi, and the third to Saraswati. The mode of celebrating may be different in various parts of India.

In the State of Bengal, the Festival of Durga Pooja is celebrated with more gaiety and passion than anywhere else in India. The large majority of Hindus in Bengal worship Mother Durga's 'fierce' aspect called Kali. According to Hindu mythology, Mother Durga had to temporarily take this 'terrifying' form in order to destroy a demon called Mahishasura. Spiritually speaking, Kali represents God's power to destroy wicked forces in order to sustain this world. The festival starts with the ritualistic sculpturing of an idol of Mother Kali using clay. The specially trained sculptor would make an addition to the statue each day, and it is totally ready by the 7th day when the festivities attain great intensity. Cities and villages are dotted with colourful and glittering pavilions adorned with Kali's idol that is set up for public Pooja every day. On the final day, the clay idol of Mother Kali is carried in the streets on beautifully decorated floats, surrounded by singing and dancing devotees. The procession ends at the banks of the river where the idol is immersed in the water. Durga Pooja also generates feverish artistic and literary activities as the celebrations are marked with dance, drama, music and poetry.

In Canada, the Bengali community celebrates Durga Pooja in a somewhat modified way. There is no procession or the immersion ceremony. The idol is stored for the next year. Cultural and religious societies set up a Pooja pavilion in a community hall where people can worship daily. The festivities reach a climax on the final day when the pavilion becomes packed with joyous devotees. People come with their families to worship and exchange greetings and gifts. The evening is concluded with cultural shows and a public feast. To give a modern touch to the festival, some organizations have started adding North American dances for their Canadian born youths. Some organizations appeal to the devotees to bring groceries for food banks.

JANMASHTAMI

This is the most important festival when Hindus celebrate the birth day of Lord Krishna. *Janmashtami* is to Hindus what

Christmas is to Christians. The word *Janmashtami* is a combination of two words- *Janma* means birth and *Ashtami* means the eighth day. The *Ashtami* refers to the eighth day of the dark fortnight of the month of Bhadraprada (August/ September) when Krishna was born. It would be a futile effort to pinpoint the year of his birth since the historicity of Hinduism itself is a highly controversial issue. However, some historians say that he lived around 900 B.C. while some Hindu scholars believe that he was born about 5200 years ago, and lived for 125 years.

Krishna was born at midnight when his father Vasudeva and mother Devaki were in prison. Devaki's demon-like brother Kansa, the king of Mathura, had imprisoned them after it was prophesied that their eighth son would be his killer. The wicked Kansa killed Devaki's seven infants soon after their birth. It is believed that when Krishna was born, miraculously, the prison guards were sleeping and the prison gate was ajar. Vasudeva secretly took Krishna to his friend Nanda and, in return, brought Nanda's newly born daughter to the prison. The next morning the cruel Kansa came to the prison and killed the baby girl. When Kansa discovered that his would-be killer had escaped, he ordered his soldiers to kill all newly born baby boys in his kingdom. However, Krishna's foster parents, Nanda and Yashoda, smuggled him out to the nearby village Vrandavan. Krishna grew up as their cowherd son, and performed many miracles at a very tender age. After foiling Kansa's many plots to kill him, eventually, Krishna slew him in a face-to-face encounter. The litany of young Krishna's adventures, miracles and exploits is too long to narrate here.

Most Hindus consider Krishna as the eighth Avatara or the incarnation of God who came to this earth to destroy wickedness and establish righteousness. To those who do not subscribe to the *Avatara* concept, Krishna was a superman with God-like attributes and powers. Some Western historians even claim that Krishna was a mythological character, and not a historical figure. Nonetheless, he has ruled the hearts and minds of all Hindus across the world for thousands of years. The chants of his name echo Hindu homes, and his images adorn the temples around the world. Both Hindus and Sikhs name their children after him. Krishna has been the subject matter for writers, poets, sculptors, painters, and intellectuals. Krishna had a multi-faceted personality, and played many roles, from the most humble to the most exalted: he was a mischievous baby boy, a herdsman, a flute player, a dancer, a divine lover, a brave warrior and king, the universal Guru, Social reformer, the greatest mediator, a counsellor, statesman, and philosopher. Above all, he was the author of Gita, one of the most sacred books of Hindus, also nicknamed as *Hindu Bible* by Christians.

Hindus across the world celebrate the birth of their divine role model and hero with fasting, worshipping and feasting. Temples and homes are decorated to welcome baby Krishna. The temples and businesses recreate scenes depicting Krishna's birth in the prison, his childhood pranks and the miracles he performed as a young boy. Mothers are busy preparing special food and sweets for the midnight family feast. People go from temple to temple offering prayers and sweets to Krishna. A colourfully decorated swinging cradle containing a doll dressed as baby Krishna is gently rocked by visiting devotees. Many people who fast and who do not have the energy to participate in the outdoor activities, quietly spend their day reading Gita or listening to devotional music. The all-day festivities reach a climax at midnight when Krishna is 'born' and welcomed in temples amidst the chanting of hymns, conch blowing, bell ringing as well as the shouting of *Victory to Lord Krishna* slogans. The joyous and noisy devotees embrace and congratulate each other. After worshipping and accepting Prasad at the temple, people return home to break their fast with a sumptuous feast.

In Canada, the Janmashtami festivities are very subdued. People who fast take a day off and spend the day at home reading Gita. Most temples stay open till midnight for visiting devotees. Religious societies and temples organize cultural shows on the closest Sunday if Janmashtami happens to fall on a working day.

RAKSHA BANDHAN

This festival is observed in the month of Shravan (July/August). Raksha Bandhan is also called with many other names- *Rakhi, Rakkhari, Salono, Rakha-mangal, Rakhouni or Rakhi-Purnima*. Literally, *Raksha* means protection, and *Bandhan* means a bond or the act of *tying a knot*. Since *tying a knot* signifies a reminder to do something, Raksha Bandhan implies reminding someone of his duty to protect somebody or something. The Guru initiates the disciple by tying a red and orange thread around the latter's right wrist which connotes that it is the duty of the disciple to protect his Guru as well as Dharma. During many other ceremonies, the officiating priest also ties the thread around the wrist of the host or the householder seeking the pledge to protect.

Later on, sisters started tying a Rakhi (a kind of a colourful bracelet made of glittery decorative threads) on their brothers or any man they wished to *adopt* as a brother. It means that the brother has the duty to protect his sister from every kind of trouble. There are many historical events signifying the importance of Rakhi as a pledge to protect. The most important one relates to Alexander the Great.

When Alexander invaded India, he faced the mighty Hindu king Pururavas. While Alexander was preparing for the decisive battle, his wife feared for his life. She had heard of the Rakhi custom and planned to use it to protect Alexander's life. She sent a Rakhi to Pururavas seeking his pledge to save her husband's life. The mighty Hindu king gave his promise. During the face-to-face sword fight, Alexander fell and became disarmed. Just as Pururavas raised his hand to slay his enemy, he noticed the Rakhi on his wrist reminding him of his pledge, and he spared Alexander's life.

On the Rakhi day, the sister and the brother before eating anything dress up in their best clothes to celebrate the occasion . She puts the auspicious vertical red mark, called *Tilak*, in the middle of his forehead, ties a Rakhi on his right wrist and offers him sweets to eat. The brother gives her a present and/or money as a symbol of his affection. If the distance makes it impossible for the sister to visit her brother to put on the Rakhi, she feels very sad and has to be content with sending a Rakhi by mail. In return, the brother sends the money by mail.

This festival offers a formal opportunity for brothers and sisters to express their respect and affection for each other and to fortify their relationship. In addition to Mother's Day and Father's Day, Canadian Hindus also celebrate Sister & Brother's Day. In modern times, Raksha Bandhan symbolizes the Canadian man's responsibility to respect women and protect their rights.

DIWALI, THE FESTIVAL OF LIGHTS

Diwali is a distortion of the Sanskrit word 'Deepavali' meaning row or cluster of lights. This most celebrated festival of Hindus is called so because of the lights that form its main characteristic. Diwali is celebrated on the new moon day of the month of Kartik (October/November).

Significance of Diwali: On Diwali night, little clay lamps are lit in Hindu homes, but now a days coloured electric lamps are also used. What is the significance of lighting a lamp? There is a logical answer to this question. It is through the light that the beauty of this world is revealed or experienced. Most civilizations of the world recognize the importance of light as a gift of God. It has always been a symbol of whatever is positive in our world of experience. To Hindus, darkness represents ignorance, and light is a metaphor for knowledge. Therefore, lighting a lamp symbolizes the destruction, through knowledge, of all negative forces- wickedness, violence, lust, anger, envy, greed, bigotry, fear, injustice, oppression and suffering, etc.

Regional interpretations and legends: The origin of this interesting festival is not known, but it has gathered a number of legends around it over the centuries. In the northern and the western regions of India, its origin is attributed to the return of Lord Rama to his kingdom after defeating the demon king Ravana. The joyous people of Ayodhya, his capital, celebrated his arrival. As already explained, Rama was the greatest of the hero-kings of India, and is also considered the seventh incarnation of Lord Vishnu.

In the eastern states, Diwali is associated with the story of Narakasura who had menaced his people with tyranny. On this day, as the legend goes, Lord Krishna killed him to free the people from oppression.

In the regions of Maharashtra and Mysore, Diwali is linked with the legendary king Bali who was immensely popular with his subjects for his generosity. However, King Bali had become arrogant and conceited, and provoked the wrath of godly people. His generosity was put to test by Lord Vishnu who appeared in the disguise of a dwarf. Lord Vishnu asked Bali for a piece of land equal to three steps. When Bali granted his wish, Lord Vishnu took the form of a super giant person, and with his two steps covered Bali's entire kingdom. With his third step he pushed Bali to the netherland. However, Lord Vishnu allowed him to visit his kingdom once a year. Since then, his people celebrated his arrival on this day, locally called *Bali Padyami*.

Historical perspective: Apart from folklores, Diwali is also associated with some important historical events. It is believed that Diwali marks the coronation of King Vikramaditya. This famous Indian king inspired many ancient tales. The era that goes by his name forty-eight year older than the Christian era.

In the modern context, Diwali also reminds Hindus of Swami Dayananda, the great reformer and the torch bearer of the Hindu renaissance during the last century, who died on this day. It is also a remembrance day for Swami Ramatirtha, the great spiritual leader who carried the message of Hindu Dharma to the western world.

A harvest festival: India enjoys two harvests a year; in the month of Kartik (October/November), the farmers harvest the second crop. Therefore, Diwali is also considered many rural Hindus to be the harvest festival when farmers offer prayers, and express their gratitude to the Almighty for the bounty they received from Him.

Festivities and fun for all: Regardless of its origin and local interpretations, Diwali is a day of fun, festivities and joy for people of all ages, throughout India. Weeks before Diwali, every Hindu family is busy painting and decorating their homes, and shopping for gifts. On the Diwali day, shops are packed with people buying freshly made sweets and fire crackers; mothers are busy preparing special dishes for the family feasts. Late evening is the time for a special Pooja (worship) at home, and illuminating the exterior of their houses with the rows of oil lamps, candles and colourful lanterns. Streets, stores and buildings are lit with electric lights and neon signs in such a way that the dark new-moon night appears to be a full-moon night. The sky is lit with fire crackers, and every street echoes with the laughter of children. People, dressed in new clothes, visit relatives and friends to exchange greetings and gifts.

The Canadian Diwali: On this joyous day, every Hindu Canadian feels homesick, and yearns for celebrating Diwali with friends and relatives left behind in the old country. They have to be satisfied with less colourful, and subdued celebrations. Since Diwali is not a public a public holiday in Canada, Many Hindus take a day off work to celebrate Diwali. Many visit the local temples and attend the special services, while some worship at home, and feast with their families. Many even dare to illuminate the front window of the house with electric lights, at the risk of inviting the comments from their non-Hindu neighbours, " Isn't it a bit early for Christmas? " To keep the Diwali spirit alive many cultural organizations and temples organize special shows and fairs. In Toronto, the Vishnu Temple, located at Highway 7 and the Yonge Street, holds the largest Diwali fair attended by thousands of Hindus from all over Ontario. Some Hindu Canadians from Guyana and Trinidad try to give a North American touch to Diwali by organizing a beauty pageant, followed by a dinner and dance. All Hindus dream for the day when Diwali will be declared a public holiday in Canada.

APPENDIX A

SOME HINDU PRAYERS

Universal

> *Om bhoor bhuvah swah, tatsavitur vareniyam bhargo devasya dheemahi dhiyo yo nah prachodayat.*

O God ! The giver of life, remover of pains and sorrows, bestower of happiness, and creator of the universe. You are most luminous, pure and adorable. We meditate on you. May you guide and inspire our intellect in the right direction.

> *Om vishwani deva savitar duritani parasuva yad bhadram tanna asuva.*

O Lord ! The creator of the universe, cleanse us of all kinds of vice and sorrows. Give us the noble qualities.

> *Om agnay naya supatha raye asman vishwani deva vayuyani viddwan. Yuyo dhyasma juhurana meno bhuyishthante namah uktim vidhema.*

O luminous God ! Lead us to the noble path of your devotion and grace. Lord ! You know all of our deeds. Cleanse us of all our vices and sins. We offer you in every way our reverence and salutation.

> *Om asato ma sad gamaya,*
> *Tamaso ma jyotir gamaya,*
> *Mrityorma amritam gamaya.*

O Lord ! Lead us from untruth to truth,
Lead us from darkness to light,
Lead us from death to immortality.

Sarway bhawantoo sukhinam,
Sarway santoo nirmayah,
Sarway bhadranee pashyantoo,
Ma kashchit dukha mapnuyat.

May all find happiness in you. May all be free from sufferings. May all realise goodness, may no one suffer from pain.

Prayer for Health

Om tanupa agne si tanvam me pahi
Om ayurda agne syayurme dehi
Om varchoda agne si varcho me dehi
Om agne yanme tanva unam tanma aprina

O Lord ! make my body healthy; give me a happy long life; make me strong; remove from my body all ailments and weakness.

Hymns for Peace

Om dyauh shanti antariksham shanti
prithvi shanti rapah shanti roshadhaya
shanti
vanaspatayah shanti vishvedeva shanti
Brahma shanti sarvam shanti shanti-reva
shanti saama shanti-redhi. Om shanti;
santi; shanti

There is peace in the heavenly region; there is peace in the atmosphere; peace reins on earth; water is calm; herbs are peace-giving; pants are peace-giving; there is harmony in the celestial objects and perfection in knowledge; everything in the universe is peaceful; peace pervades everywhere. May that peace come to me !

Family Welfare

> ***Om anuvratah pituh putro matra bhavatoo sammanah. Jaya patye-madhu matim wacham wadhatoo shantiwam.***
> ***Om ma Bhrata bhrataram dwikshan ma swasara muta swasa. Samyanchah savrata bhootwa wacham vadata bhadraya.***
> ***Om samani prapa sahawo' nna bhagah samanay yoktre sahawo yunajmi. samyancho gnim saparyatara nabhi miwa bhitah.***

O supreme and merciful Lord ! We, the members of this family, have gathered here to offer you our prayers. Grant us wisdom understanding for promoting mutual love and affection. May there be no hatred, and may we be in harmony with each other. May we treat each other and everbody else with justice, love and empathy. May the younger members of this family be polite, respectful and dutiful, and may all be truthful and sweet.

O merciful Father ! Free us from diseases and stress, and help us enjoy a healthy life of hundred years. May we work with cooperation in all undertakings. May we earn our livelihood hoestly, and share our earnings with others.

May we have good relations with our neighbours and members of the community. May our mind lead us to the path of righteousness, and develope the spirit of truthfulness, service and cooperation in us.

Meal time prayer

Om annpatay annasya no dehyana miwasya shushminah; prapradataram tarisha urjam no dhehi dwipaday chatuspaday.

O Lord, the provider of food ! May you give us healthy and energy producing food. Give happiness to those who give charity. May all living beings be pleased with energy-producing food.

Courtesy: **Veda Niketan,**
Durban,
South Africa

APPENDIX B

HINDU TEMPLES AND ORGANIZATIONS IN CANADA

BRITISH COLUMBIA

Vishwa Hindu Parishad
3885 Albert Street
Burnaby, B.C. V3V 2C8 Phone: 604-299-5922

Hare Krishna Temple
5462, S.E. Marine Drive
Burnaby, B.C. V5J 3G8 Phone: 604-844-7221

Shiv Mandir
1795 Napier Street
Vancouver, B.C. V5L 2N1 Phone: 604-254-2624

Maha Lakshmi Temple
11th. Avenue (Nr. Fraser St.)
Vancouver, B.C. Phone: 604-874-0175

ALBERTA

Hindu Society of Calgary
2225 24th Avenue, N.E.
Calgary, AB., Phone: 403-291-2551

Radha Madhava Cultural Centre
313, 4th Street, N.E.
Calgary, AB., T2E 3S3 Phone: 403-265-3302

Mahaganapathi Temple
1403-111th Street
Edmonton, AB.,

Hindu Society of Alberta
14225-133 Avenue
Edmonton, AB., T5L 4W3 Phone: 403-451-5130

SASKATCHEWAN

Sri Lakhmi Narayan Temple
107 La Ronge Road
Saskatoon, SK., S7K 5T3 Phone: 306-933-4041

Hare Krishna Temple
1279 Retallack Street
Regina, SK., S4T 2H8 Phone: 306-781-2381

MANITOBA

Manitoba Arya Samaj
485 Maryland Street
Winnipeg, Man., R3G 1M4
Contact: Haripal Rajpal Phone: 204-783-7785

ONTARIO
METROPOLITAN TORONTO & VICINITY (EAST)

Hare Krishna Temple
243 Avenue Road
Toronto, Ont., M5R 2J6 Phone: 416-922-5415

Hindu Prarthana Samaj
62 Fern Avenue
Toronto, Ont., M6R 1K1 Phone: 416-536-9229

Shantiniketan Vidya Mandir
475 Cosburn Avenue
Toronto, Ont., M4J 2N6
Contact: Prof. Adesh Phone: 416-281-1904

Sri Chinmoy Meditation Centre
1085 Bathurst Street
Toronto, Ont., M5R 3G8
Contact: Shivaram Trichur Phone: 416-532-2560

Bharatiya Cultural Association of Ont.
205 Sorauren Avenue
Toronto, Ont., M6R 2G1
Contact: Lallubhai Patel Phone: 416-532-0239

Shiva Mandir
205 Champagne Drive, Unit 1
Toronto, Ont. M3J 2C6 Phone: 416-751-6133

Bharat Sevashram Sangha
196 Royal York Road
Toronto, Ont., M8V 2V6 Phone: 416-252-6658

Satya Sanatan Dharma Cultural Sabha
19 Crane Avenue,
Weston, Ont., M9P 1V1
Contact: Harry Sahu Phone: 416-889-0621

Hindu Solidarity Mission
262 Barnhill Road
Maple, Ont., LOJ 1EO
Contact: Ramesh Misra Phone: 416-832-7099

Swami Narayan Hindu Mission
32-246 Brookfort Drive
Etobicoke, Ont., M9W 6W2
Contact: Naresh Patel Phone: 416-840-4985

Sanatan Dharma Satsang
5 Winterset Crescent
Etobicoke, Ont., M9R 4A1
Contact: Deo Kernahan Phone: 416-241-5848

Canadian Vedic Sabha &
Cultural Organization
P.O. Bx 2596, Station S
Scarborough, Ont., M1W 7K0
Contact: Lalan K. Jani Phone: 416-884-2050

Kaival Gyan Sampradaya
56 Wharton Square
Scarborough, Ont., M1V 4N5
Contact: Mahendra Patel Phone: 416-299-5355

Arya Samaj, Toronto
P.O. Bx 57
Agincourt Postal Station
Scarborough, Ont., M1S 3B4
Contact: Amar Erry Phone: 416-471-1211

Jai Durga Hindu Society
2691 Markham Road, Unit 5
Scarborough, Ont., M1X 1M4
Contact: Al Gogna Phones: 416-297-1146 / 416-754-2883

Chinmaya Mission of Toronto
100 Cooperwood Square
Scarborough, Ont., M1V 2C1
Contact: Charanjeev Dewan Phone: 146-291-3862

The Voice of Dharma Cultural Society
214 John Tabor Trail
Scarborough, Ont., M1D 2R4
Contact: D. Raghbeer Phone: 416-283-6068

Vedic Religious Assembly
131 Ingleton Blvd.
Scarborough, Ont
M1V 2Y3
Contact: Pt. Chandan Prasad Phone: 416-293-3847

Shri Anandpur Holy Satsang Ashram
260 Ingleton Blvd.
Scarborough, Ont., M1V 3R1 Phone: 416—291-3954

Hindu Cultural Society
1940 Ellesmere Road, Unit 7
Scarborough, Ont.,
Contacts: Mahendra Gupta Phone: 416-269-6777

Gayatri Pariwar-Yug Nirman
P.O. Box 98, Agincourt Station
Scarborough, Ont., M1S 3B4
Contact: Chimanbhai Patel Phone: 416-293-9005

Toronto Arya Samaj
29 New Forest Square
Scarborough, Ont., M1V 2Z6
Contact: Anand Rupnarain Phone: 416-299-0188

Federation of Gujarati Associations
58 Clarke Avenue
Thornhill, Ont., L3T 1S5
Contact: Bhagubhai Patel Phone: 416-740-8000

Gujarati Cultural Society of Toronto
134 Rimmington Drive
Thornhill, Ont., L4J 6K2
Contact: Chhibubhai Bhana Phone: 416-738-0709

Vishnu Mandir
Voice of Vedas Cultural Sabha
8640 Yonge Street
Thornhill, Ont., L4J 1W8
Contact: Dr. B. Doobay Phone: 416-827-8488 / 416-886-1724

Ganesh Temple
Hindu Temple Society of Canada
10945 Bayview Avenue
Richmond Hill, Ont., M4A 2N9
Contact: S. Venkatraman Phone: 416-425-8720

Gujurat Samaj of Toronto
14 Upton Crescent
Markham, Ont., L3R 3T4
Contact: Kanitbhai Patel Phone: 416-731-1625

Swaminarayan Bhakti Mandal
71 Forbes Crescent
Markham, Ont., L3R 6S7
Contact: Indrakant Patel Phone: 416-470-7598

Canadian Council of Hindus
71 Forbes Crescent
Markham, Ont., L3R 6S7 Phone: 416-513-6582

Toronto Kalibari
1441 Rose Bank Road
Pickering, Ont., L1V 1P3
Contact: P.P. Bannerjee Phone: 416-837-5426

Devi Temple
2590 Brock Road
Pickering, Ont., L1V 2P8
Contact: Srikant Acharya Phone: 416-686-8534

PEEL & HALTON

Hindu Sabha
P.O. 2092
Brampton, Ont., L6T 3S3 Tel. 416-459-7984

Geeta Ashram of Toronto
2 Morton Way
Brampton, Ont., L6Y 2R7
Contact: Kamal Lohra Phone: 416-452-1996

Peel Arya Samaj
22 Maple Hurst Square
Brampton, Ont., L6Z 1J6
Contact: Jai Brijpaul

Arya Samaj Mississauga
Box 242, Postal Station A
Mississauga, Ont., L5A 3A1
Contact: C.P. Gupta Phone: 416-828-0874

Vedantic Cultural Society
3632 Molly Avenue
Mississauga, Ont., L5A 3M5
Contact: Paul Sharma Phone: 416-566-5574

Vishwa Hindu Parishad (Ont)
Box 2318, Square One Station P
Mississauga, Ont. L5B 3C8

Satya Jyoti Cultural Sabha
505 Menton Court
Mississauga, Ont., L5R 2Z6
Contact: K. Nandkishore Phone: 416-568-3620

Vaishnu Devi Temple
3259 Bronte (Highway 25)
Oakville, Ont., L6J 4Z3 Phone: 416-825-4202

Arya Samaj Burlington
1092 Maplehurst Avenue
Burlington, Ont., L7T 3G4
Contact: V. Kapila Phone: 416-632-8597

Chinmaya Cultural Organization
129 Appleby Place
Burlington, Ont., L7L 2X2
Contact: Sneh Chakraburty Phone: 416-637-7448

SOUTH-WEST ONTARIO

Hindu Samaj Temple (Hamilton)
6297 Twenty Road East
Hannon, Ont., L0R 1P0, Phone: 416-679-6935

Niagara Hindu Samaj
18 Golden Blvd.
St. Catherines Ont., L2N 7L9
Contact: Mrs. Kamlesh Sharma Phone: 416-646-1166

Radha-Krishna Mandir
67 Old Mill Road
Cambridge, Ont., N3H 4R8
Contact: Dwarka Persaud Ph: 519-650-1575 / 519-748-4586

Brahma Rishi Mission
448 Lancaster Street West
Kitchener, Ont., N2H 4V9 Phone: 519-579-1486

Hindu Cultural Centre
138 St. Bees Close
London, Ont., N6G 4A6
Contact: P.L. Gupta Phone: 519-674-6808

London Arya Samaj
43 Beachmount Crescent
London, Ont., N6E 2J2
Contact: Pt. Balram Prashad

Vedic Study Circle Windsor
315 Cabana Road East
Windsor, Ont., N9G 1A1

OTTAWA & CARLTON REGION

Arya Samaj Ottawa
149 Sai Crescent
Ottawa, Ont., K1G 5P2
Contact: B. Gandhi Phone: 613-738-2752

Hare Krishna Temple
212 Somerset Street East
Ottawa, Ont., K1N 6V4 Phone: 613-565-6544

Hindu Temple of Ottawa-Carlton
4835 Bank Street (Hwy. 31)
Gloucester, Ont., K1G 3N4 Ph: 613-822-6008 / 822-1531

QUEBEC

Montreal Arya Samaj
307-5311 Sherbrook West
Montreal, Que., H4A 1V3
Contact: V. Jagannath

Hindu Mission of Canada Temple
955 Belle Chasse Street
Montreal, Que., H2S 1Y2
Contact: Kamal Narayan Sharma Phone: 514-270-5557

Hare Krishna Temple
1626, Pie IX Blvd.
Montreal, Que. H1V 2C5

NOVA SCOTIA

Hindu Sanstha of Nova Scotia
P.O. Box 468
Port Hawkesbury, N.S., B03 2V0
(Temple Location: Aulds Cove)
Contact: Dr. Joshi Phone: 902-863-4866

Vedanta Society Temple
6421 Cork Street
Halifax, N.S., B3L 1Z5
Contact: Ravi Dogra Phone: 902-876-2124

NEWFOUNDLAND

Chinmaya Mission (St. John's)
P.O. Box 13603, Station A
St. John's, Nfld., A1B 1G4
Contact: Dr. S.P. Reddy Phone: 709-722-5731

APPENDIX C

POPULATION OF HINDUS IN VARIOUS COUNTRIES

Afghanistan	120,000
Algeria	500
Argentina	2,000
Australia	45,000
Austria	5,000
Bahrain	20,000
Bangladesh	11,000,000
Barbados	100
Belgium	5,000
Bhutan	62,000
Botswana	5,000
Brazil	50
Britain	1,000,000
Brunei	500
Cameroon	50
Canada	320,000
Central African Republic	20
Chad	20
Czechoslovakia, the former	100
Chile	20
China	50
Columbia	50
Congo	100
Cuba	100
Denmark	5,000
Egypt	5,000
Equador	500
Ethiopia	2,000
Fiji	600,000
Finland	100
France	5,000
Gabon	100

Gambia	500
Germany	34,000
Ghana	500
Guinea	50
Guyana	400,000
Hong Kong	82,000
Hungary	50
Iceland	6
India	760,750,000
Indonesia	5,000,000
Iran	10,000
Iraq	5,000
Ireland	20
Israel	100
Italy	200
Ivory Coast	1,000
Jamaica	20,000
Japan	5,200
Jordan	1,000
Kenya	60,000
Kuwait	10,000
Laos	500
Liberia	500
Madagascar	1,000
Malawi	2,000
Malaysia	1,095,000
Mauritius	600,000
Mayanmar	7,100,000
Mexico	20
Morocco	50
Mozambique	500
Nepal	20,000,000
Netherlands	150,000
New Zealand	40,000
Nigeria	22,000
Norway	1,000
Pakistan	1,100,000
Panama	500
Phillipines	1,000
Poland	100

Portugal	5,000
Qatar	500
Reunion Island	250,000
Russia	1,500
Saudi Arabia	5,000
Senegal	100
Seychelles	500
Sierra Leone	500
Singapore	145,000
Somalia	5,000
South Africa	580,000
South Korea	50
South Yemen	5,000
Spain	10,000
Sri Lanka	2,500,000
Sudan	500
Suriname	300,000
Switzerland	5,000
Syria	100
Tanzania	60,000
Thailand	6,000
Trinidad	200,000
Tunisia	100
Turkey	100
Uganda	16,000
United Arab Emirates	15,000
United States	560,000
Upper Volta	100
Vietnam	5,000
Yugoslavia, the former	5,000
Zambia	16,000
Zimbabwe	4,000

Courtesy: **Hinduism Today**
Himalayan Academy
Concord, California

REFERENCES

Chapter 1

"Invasion or Indigenous?". Hinduism Today November 1991: 13.

Sen, K.M. Hinduism. Harmondsworth Middlesex, Penguin Books Limited, 1975.

Frawley, David. Gods, Sages and Kings. Salt Lake City: Passage Press, 1991.

Bhattacharya, N.N. Ancient Indian History and Civilization. Columbia (U.S.A.): South Asia Publications, 1988.

Chapter 2

Bhattacharya, N.N. Ancient Indian History. Columbia: South Asia Publications 1988.

Jayaswal, Hindu Polity Part I & II. Bangalore, India: The Bangalore Printing & Publications, 1943.

Thapar, Romila A history of India. London, England:Penguin Group, 1966.

Basham, A.L The Wonder that Was India, New York: Hawthorn Books Inc. 1963.

Vadalankar, Nardev Spiritual teachings of Hinduism Durban. S.A., 1985.

Chapter 3

Bhattacharya, N.N. Ancient Indian History. Columbia: South Asia Publications, 1988.

Thapar, Romila. A History of India. London, England:Penguin Group, 1966.

Basham, A.L. The wonder that Was India: New York, U.S.A.Hawthorn Books Inc., 1963.

Vedalankar, Nardev A Concise Study of Hindu Scriptures Durban, S.A: Veda Niketan, 1985.

Ketkar, S.V. History of Caste in India. Delhi: Low Price Publications, 1990.

Saraswati, Sawmi Dayananda. Light of Hope. (Satyarth Prakash) New Delhi: Sarvadeshik Arya Pratinidhi Sabha

Chapter 4

Patel, Ishwarbhai. Sciences and the Vedas. New Delhi, India:Somaiya Publications Pvt. Ltd., 1984.

Vedalankar, Nardev. Spiritual Teachings of Hinduism .Durban: Veda Niketan, 1985.

Salem, Semaan and Kumar, Alok. Said al-Andalusi's Science in the Medieval World: Book of the Categories of Nations. Austin, Texas: University of Texas Press, 1991.

Chapter 5

"Did the Hindus Discover America?" Star India, March 20, 1992.

Muthanna, I. M. People of India in North America Bangalore, India: 1982.

Buchignani, Norman et al. Continuous Journey. Toronto: McClelland & Stewart Ltd., 1985.

Chapter 6

Buchignani, Norman et al. Continuous Journey. Toronto: McClelland & Stewart Ltd., 1985.

Mukherjee. Alok K. (Edt.) East Indians: Myths And Reality Toronto: Indian Immigrant Aid Services, 1978.

Subramaniam, Indira A. et al. Papers on the East Indian Community, Ontario Ministry of Culture and Recreation, 1977.

Chapter 7

Vedalankar, Nardev, A Concise Study of Hindu Scriptures Durban, S.A: Veda Niketan, 1985.

Naidoo, Joshephine C, "Women of South Asian Origins Status of Research, Problems, Future, Issues" The South Asian Diaspora in Canada: Six Essay, ed. Milton, Israel. (Toronto: The Multicultural History Society of Onytario, 1987: 41-42.

Chapter 8

Raman, V.V. "Hindu Marriage System." INDHER July-August, 1981: 316.

Chapter 9

Vedalankar, Nardev A concise study of Hindu Scriptures Durban, S.A: Veda Niketan, 1985.

Thapar, Romila. A History of India. London, England: Penguin Group, 1966.

Menon, I.A. "The Hindu Scriptures." Hindu Dharma Review December, 1987: 7.

Chapter 10 & 11

Vedalankar, Nardev. Essential Teachings of Hinduism. Durban, S.A: Veda Niketan, 1979.

Ross, Floyd and Hills, Tynette. The Great Religions bywhich Men Live. U.S.A: Fawcett Premier Books, 1956.

Subramuniyaswami, Gurudeva Sivaya. 9 Questions People Ask About Hinduism. Hanamaulu, HI: Himalayan Academy.

Kishore, B.R. Hinduism. Delhi, India: Diamond Pocket Book,

Viswanathan, Ed. Daddy, Am I A Hindu? Bombay, India: Bhartiya Vidya Bhavan, 1988.

Vedalankar, Nardev. Shastra Navanitam: A Concise StudyOf Hindu Scriptures. Durban, S.A: Veda Niketan, 1985.

Murthy, B. Srinivasa. The Bhagavad Gita. Long Beach, CA:Long Beach Publication, 1985.

Talreja, Kanayalal M. Philosophy of Vedas. Bombay, India:Talreja Publication, 1982.

Chapter 12 & 13

Chinmayananda, Swami. Art of God symbolism. Bombay: Central Chinmaya Mission Trust.

Vedalankar, Nardev. "Our Religious Symbols"-Veda Jyoti. June, 1990: 5.

Chapter 14

The Theosophical Society. Sanatana-Dharma.Madras: The Theosophical Publishing House, 1980.

Nathan, R.S., ed. Symbolism in Hidnuism. Bombay: Central Chinmaya Mission Trust, 1983.

Narain, Shakun. Hindu Customs and Beliefs. Bombay: Bhartiya Vidya Bhavan, 1987.

Vedalankar, Pandit Nardev. Essential Teachings of Hinduism.Durban S.A: Veda Niketan, Arya Partinidhi Sabha, 1979

Chapter 15.

Kishore, B.R. Hinduism. New Delhi: Diamond Pocket Books,

Nathan, R.S., ed. Symbolism in Hidnuism. Bombay: Central Chinmaya Mission Trust, 1983.

Vedalankar, Pandit Nardev. Essential Teachings of Hinduism. Durban S.A: Veda Niketan, Arya Partinidhi Sabha, 1979

Rajhans, Gyan. "Janmashtami Greetings." Hindu Dharma Review July, 1987: 5.

Upadhyay, Madhav. "Raksha Bandhan." Hindu Dharma Review July, 1987: 18.

Adhopia, Ajit. "Diwali- "The Festival of Lights." Hindu Dharma Review July-Sept. 1989: 5

Rajhans, Gyan. "Shivaratri" Hindu Dharma Review Jan.-March 1989: 12.

Rajhans, Gyan. "Nava-Ratri" Hindu Dharma Review April 1987: 12.

Vishnu

Lakshmi

Vishnu Temple, Thornhill [Ont.]

Hindu Samaj Temple, Hamilton [Ont.]

Hindu Temple of Ottawa-Carleton

Vedic Cultural Centre, Arya Samaj, Toronto [Ont.]

Hindu Sabha, Brampton [Ont.]

ERRATUM

The publisher regrets the typographical misprints that are outlined below with the appropriate corrections:

Page	Line	Misprint	Correction
IX	24	colos	colours
XIV	26	suchsilly	such silly
XIV	34	Sankritized	Sanskritized
XV	7	startedreading	started reading
XV	27	culture	cultural
XV	33	voluntaryassistance	voluntary assistance
XV	34	incompleting	in completing
6	24	indicates	indicate
9	16	interegration	integration
43	4	Malasia	Malaysia
43	12	Suriname	Surinam
53	1	Advertise	*Advertiser*
59	9	stereotyp	stereotype
64	16	harrassment	harassment
64	18	harrassement	harassment
69	37	surprize	surprise
78	1	balance	balanced
87	4	*ainted*	*tainted*
88	18	Jones	Joneses
124	10	satifaction	satisfaction
128	14	waives	waves
158	29	divout	devout
164	32	grooms	groom's
172	4	surprize	surprise
163	35	process	procession
181	7	sister	sister's